Dragons, Grasshoppers, & Frogs!

Dragons, Grasshoppers, & Frogs!

A Pocket Guide To The Book Of Revelation For Teenagers And Newbies!

Jerry L. Parks

Weekly Reader Press
New York Lincoln Shanghai

Dragons, Grasshoppers, & Frogs!
A Pocket Guide To The Book Of Revelation For Teenagers And Newbies!

Copyright © 2005 by Jerry L. Parks

Weekly Reader Press
an imprint of iUniverse, Inc.
and the Weekly Reader Corporation

iUniverse books may be ordered through booksellers or by contacting:

iUniverse
2021 Pine Lake Road, Suite 100
Lincoln, NE 68512
www.iuniverse.com
1-800-Authors (1-800-288-4677)

Scripture used is from _Holy Bible, The New Living Translation,_
Copyright © 1996 by Tyndale Charitable Trust.
Used by permission of Tyndale House Publishers.
All rights reserved.

ISBN-13: 978-0-595-36668-2
ISBN-10: 0-595-36668-6

Printed in the United States of America

Contents

Dragons, Grasshoppers, & Frogs!

You're about to begin a strange and wonderful journey. It will be a journey with sharp curves and many dark valleys. Along the way, you'll see some of the strangest things you've ever seen in your life. You'll meet seven-headed beasts rising from the sea, and dragons falling from the sky. You'll see cities of earth crumbling to the ground, and a city from Heaven coming down to the earth! You visit both Heaven and Hell, and see people who can't die. Above all, you'll discover the revelation or unveiling of Jesus Christ as King of Kings and Lord of Lords. That's what *Revelation* is all about.

Revelation has twenty-two chapters, four hundred and four verses, and about twelve thousand words. It's about the future of Planet Earth. This handbook on *Revelation* is meant to be just that—a handbook. It's not meant to be an in-depth study of every detail. There are many other books for that. If you decide to do a deeper study, check out *The Complete Idiot's Guide to the Book of Revelation* (Alpha Publishers) by James Bell and Stan Campbell, or *Revelation: God's Word for the Biblically Inept* (Starburst Publishers) by Daymond Duck. These are great books, and will lead you to many others!

Before we start, some things must be considered. These are important to understand what God is saying, and they are important to your spiritual life.

First, the most important thing God wants you to know is the Plan of Salvation. Do you *know* you're a Christian? HOW do you know? Here's what God says about salvation:

Salvation's plan—The theme of *Revelation* is salvation. That means to be saved from your sins. Although *Revelation* is full of destruction, God's desire is to save, not destroy. If you don't know whether or not you're saved (a Christian), you probably aren't. Do you know for sure where you're going when you die? A person who doesn't know where they're going is lost. Salvation is easy for you, but it cost God the life of His Son. To be saved, you need to:

1. Realize you're not the perfect and holy person God requires in order to spend forever with Him in Heaven. Anything less than God's perfection is called *sin*, and sin requires *death*. (See Rom. 3:23.)

2. Understand that the *only* way to be perfect in His sight is to be perfect in His Son. No good deeds that you can do will make you *that* perfect (Isa. 64:6). So God sent Jesus Christ to take your place when He died on the cross in order that you could share *His* place—Heaven—forever. (See Rom. 6:23.)

3. Pray now and ask God to forgive you for your sinfulness and save you through His Son Jesus. Tell Him you understand that sinners deserve Hell, and you know you have no hope of heaven without accepting Jesus into your heart. God will save you. (See Rom. 10:13.)

Next, there are some things you need to understand in the book of *Revelation*. These will help you get off to a good start. They are:

The End of the World—isn't!—Everyone talks about the end of the world, but *Revelation* shows us that it will be more like the end of history—at least history as we know it! Revelation is also about the end of sin, death, the devil, the world economic systems, world religion, etc. Every person has a soul that will spend forever somewhere. Even after the terrible destruction in *Revelation*, God creates a new Heaven and a new earth, so the world really doesn't completely end!

Jesus is God—All through *Revelation*, we see Jesus—not as the man who walked the dusty streets of Jerusalem and was crucified 2000 years ago—but as the Son of God. Keep this picture of Jesus in your mind. While we may not understand how He can be God and the Son of God, just remember—Jesus is the powerful Creator of all things, and *Revelation* shows how He'll return to take back the earth someday! (See John 1:1-3.)

Jesus is the focus of Revelation—Don't get hung up on dragons, grasshoppers, frogs, beasts, or the devil. Jesus Christ, and His coming to earth in all His glory, is the important message *Revelation*. Never forget that!

Symbols must be explained carefully—As you read *Revelation*, John will show you all sorts of weird creatures. You'll see locusts with long hair, spirits that look like frogs, beasts rising out of the sea, and dragons with seven heads! John describes what he sees, and he doesn't understand everything anymore than you do. Usually the Bible explains itself, so *Revelation* isn't that hard to interpret. While the symbols may seem strange to us today, they will be easily understood when the events of *Revelation* take place!

Interpretations can differ—In studying God, sometimes good people disagree on things. In studying *Revelation*, people have always disagreed on exactly what it means, and especially on an event called *the Rapture*. Rapture means *to take something*, and it means Jesus taking Christians to Heaven. The big disagreement people have is when this is going to happen—before, during, or after the terrible Great Tribulation period described in *Revelation*. In *Dragons, Grasshoppers, & Frogs!*, we will take the position that Jesus will return to take all true Christians to Heaven *before* this period. It's hard to imagine Christ leaving His children on earth to suffer this terrible period of punishment.

Numbers are important, but don't get too caught up in them—There are numbers all through the book, such as 12, 144,000, 666, 12,000, and 1260. While all of these are important, you'll do fine to simply remember that the number '7' almost always means 'completion', and that's what this book is all about. God completes His plan for planet Earth!

There are blessings for reading—There's a special blessing on you for reading and obeying the things written in *Revelation*. Always remember this promise! *Revelation* is a very special book. However, God did put it last in the Bible for a reason. He wants you to be familiar with the books that come before it, too! *Revelation* is meant to be read and studied, not sealed up and hidden! Don't let anyone tell you this book isn't meant to be understood!

The Bible comes full circle—It's interesting that the Bible comes full circle in what it shows us from *Genesis* to *Revelation*. For example, in Genesis we see mankind begin in a paradise with God. That's also how *Revelation* ends. In Genesis, we see the Tree of Life. We see it once more in *Revelation*. In *Genesis* we see what life was like before the devil brought sin into the world. In *Revelation*, we see sin and the devil gone forever. In *Genesis* we see the beginning of sorrow, suffering and death. In *Revelation*, we see the end of all three! *Genesis* and *Revelation*—two beautiful bookends that hold together the rest of the Bible!

Now let's look at the way *Dragons, Grasshoppers, & Frogs!* is organized:

Revelation is easy to outline (see 1:19). It is divided into three sections, all focusing on *Jesus*—the key to the book:

The *Person* of Jesus—His heavenly *glory!* (1:1-1:20)

The *People* of Jesus—His *instructions* to us! (2:1-3:22)

The *Plan* of Jesus—His *plans* for the world! (4:1-22:21)

To make your trip through *Revelation* more comfortable, each chapter of the book is broken down into bite-size portions. Each chapter of *Revelation* is listed for you. The verses are taken from the *New Living Translation* and placed at the start of each chapter. Following the Scripture, you'll notice:

Explained in a nutshell!—In this section, the chapter is summarized in a nutshell. This section simply gives you a brief overview of the chapter.

Key verse—Every verse in *Revelation* is important. Some, however, are keys. The key verse might be one you commit to memory from each chapter!

Key word—Like key verses, some words are simply keys to chapters. The key words are words you might circle and try to learn why they were chosen as keys!

Focus locus—themes and threads throughout!—Listed here will be sub-themes that weave throughout *Revelation*. These help you keep the *big picture* of the book continually before your eyes!

Getting to know Jesus!—Never forget that the title of this book is The *Revelation* of Jesus Christ! *Revelation* unveils or reveals the glory of Jesus and His return to earth. Jesus is mentioned by many names in the book, and each one is listed. These names should help you learn much more about who Jesus is, and what Jesus is doing today!

Nuts to crack—terms to know!—Here, each important word in each chapter is listed and defined for you. This is kind of a *vocab lab* where you'll learn just what the chapter is all about. Look up other definitions of these words in a good Bible dictionary or encyclopedia. Locate them elsewhere in your Bible.

Get to know the meaning of these words—they are defined to help you understand the real meaning of *Revelation*!

Backpack for the road—Principles to Ponder!—How many times have you ever asked: *'So, what's this got to do with me?'* In this section, you'll take what you've read and what you've learned, and hit the road of life! Bring to your world the lessons and principles each chapter teaches you, and use them in your life for the entire world to see. This is how you grow in your Christian faith!

Journal for the journey—My reflections!—This final section is for you to reflect on where you are in your Christian growth. Many of these questions will show you where you need to grow more in your spiritual life. Here's where you should keep a separate journal, and make special notes to yourself on how you're maturing as a Christian!

Before we start, let's pick up some keys for unlocking the wonderful secrets of *Revelation*.

Revelation 'rules for the road'!

1. *Revelation—and the whole Bible—is God's Word.* Every verse.

2. *Let the Bible interpret the Bible.* If we make up our opinions along the way, we'll never be sure who's right. We have a little room to guess, but very little. (II Pet. 1:20)

3. *Pray as you study Revelation.* God does promise you a blessing for studying this book, but the devil hates it! Why? *Revelation* shows his defeat. Pray as you study!

4. *Study Revelation seriously.* Set aside a time to give your undivided attention to this important book. Keep your Bible by your side and don't be afraid to mark in it.

5. *Put Revelation into action.* Studying the Bible without putting into action what you learn isn't effective study. That's why 'Backpack for Road' furnishes life principles to take with you to school and elsewhere. Learn from the book. Live it in life.

6. *Tie Revelation to the daily news.* When you see and hear of earthquakes, Israel, wars, famine, the Euphrates River area, etc., remember—these will take front and center stage during the events of *Revelation*. Get familiar with the news events. *Revelation* gives you previews of coming attractions!

7. *Understand Revelation's background.* The book was written by John—one of the closest disciples of Jesus— around 90 AD. By this time, John was a very old man. He wrote this book to tell Christians of his day—and today—what must take place on earth before Jesus comes back. *Revelation* isn't a happy story. It just has a happy ending—the devil loses, and Christ wins.

There are seven theme-threads that run through *Revelation*, tying it and everything together. These threads are the super-subjects of the book. You'll study each in much more detail as you go through *Revelation*. Keep a close eye on these theme-threads as you study:

The thread of *earth and all creation*—God created the earth and everything in it. God didn't use the 'big bang' theory or evolution to do this. God put mankind on earth to enjoy it and care for it. But mankind disobeyed God and brought sin and death into God's world. God loves our earth, and He won't let man destroy it through pollution, global warming, or nuclear bombs. God will eventually bring the earth back to the world He intended—that process is what *Revelation* is all about. (See Isa. 35.)

The thread of *Antichrist*—You'll meet in *Revelation* the devil's finest accomplishment. He'll be more evil than Hitler, and will lead the world from peace into the most terrible period history has ever known (II Thes. 2:7-10). He is seen as riding the white horse of peace, but this will be a trick. As evil as he may be in his heart, he'll fool the people of the world and be worshipped as a god.

The thread of *Satan & evil*—The old devil has been around since time began, but did you know he was once a good angel? (See Isa. 14:12-15.) In *Revelation*, you'll see the devil working harder than he ever has because he knows his time will be running out. Satan and his demons are the force behind the evil, destruction, and terrorism you see in the world today. As evil as the world seems today, it's nothing next to the evil that's coming. The time of *Revelation* will be a hard time for those who decide to worship the true God.

The thread of *tribulation, sorrow, and death*—Tribulation means *great trouble*, and that's what the world is in for just before Jesus comes back to the earth. Sin in our world has always brought trouble, suffering, and death, but as the end of history gets closer, things will get much worse. This period is called the Great Tribulation (Matt. 24:21), and it will last 7 years.

The thread of *Jesus as King*—Jesus is God, the Son of God, and the Creator of all things. He came to earth 2000 years ago to live and die as a human being and—as God—to pay for your sins. But a king needs a kingdom, and Earth is the kingdom of Christ. Today earth is full of sin, and until earth is redeemed from sin the King is a king in waiting. The events of *Revelation* describe the process of redeeming (buying back) the earth from sin. It will be a painful process for humankind. But the King will return (Matt. 24:27-31) to set up His kingdom. As a Christian, you'll have a part in Christ's rule! (See John 1:1-3.)

The thread of *salvation and redemption*—Redemption means to buy back something that was lost. Redemption of mankind and the earth itself is the subject of *Revelation*. Redemption is only accomplished by blood and death (Rev. 12:11). That's why God let people in the Old Testament kill a lamb in place of sinful persons. Then Jesus came as the perfect Lamb of God to die for sins. The terrible events of *Revelation* will cause the shedding of more blood than all the wars of history combined. Mankind—which has rejected the blood of Christ—will spill his own blood at the end of history. (See Luke 21:28.)

The thread of *Israel*—Israel is the land of the Jews. Look on a map, and Israel appears almost at the center of the world. It's the small country in the Middle East whose people were known as the Hebrews in the Old Testament. Jerusalem was and is the most famous city in Israel. Israel is always in the news today. Israel is also the nation God keeps closest to His heart, since His Son Jesus was born a Jew. Because God loves Israel in a special way, the devil has a unique hate for that country. God promised to bless everyone who blesses Israel, and curse all its enemies (Genesis 12). Right now, the United States is one of the few friends Israel has in the world. God is watching how America treats that small nation! The Jewish people have suffered throughout history, the most well-known suffering being the Holocaust, Hitler's murder of more than 6 million Jews in Europe. In *Revelation*, Israel will suffer as it has never suffered before. Yet God will protect Israel. In the end, Jesus Christ will make Jerusalem the capital of His Kingdom!

How should I use *Dragons, Grasshoppers, & Frogs!*?

- ✓ Begin your reading with prayer. *Revelation* is a very special book that takes God's leading to understand.

- ✓ Browse through the whole book fist. Get a feel for the terms and ideas in *Revelation*.

- ✓ Keep your Bible close. Although the verses are printed here, other translations will help give you a different slant on some of the words.

- ✓ Go through the book chronologically. Study *Revelation* in the order it was written.

- ✓ Look up cross-references. There are many cross references in *Dragons, Grasshoppers, & Frogs!*. They are in parenthesis. Look them up in your Bible.

- ✓ Look up *Revelation* cross references. If you are referenced to another chapter after a term or principle, try to locate the similar word or idea. It may not be the identical word or idea but it's cross-referenced for a reason.

OK—are you ready to start on your journey through *Revelation?* Hang on to your hat! It's going to be a wild ride!

Chapter 1

"Setting the Stage for the End of the Age!" (Or, 'you mean there's not *really* going to be an end of the world?!')

This is a revelation from Jesus Christ, which God gave him concerning the events that will happen soon. An angel was sent to God's servant John so that John could share the revelation with God's other servants. *2*John faithfully reported the word of God and the testimony of Jesus Christ—everything he saw. *3*God blesses the one who reads this prophecy to the church, and he blesses all who listen to it and obey what it says. For the time is near when these things will happen. *4*This letter is from John to the seven churches in the province of Asia. Grace and peace from the one who is, who always was, and who is still to come; from the sevenfold Spirit before his throne; *5*and from Jesus Christ, who is the faithful witness to these things, the first to rise from the dead, and the commander of all the rulers of the world. All praise to him who loves us and has freed us from our sins by shedding his blood for us. *6*He has made us his Kingdom and his priests who serve before God his Father. Give to him everlasting glory! He rules forever and ever! Amen! *7*Look! He comes with the clouds of Heaven. And everyone will see him—even those who pierced him. And all the nations of the earth will weep because of him. Yes! Amen! *8*"I am the Alpha and the Omega—the beginning and the end," says the Lord God. "I am the one who is, who always was, and who is still to come, the Almighty One." *9*I am John, your brother. In Jesus we are partners in suffering and in the Kingdom and in patient endurance. I was exiled to the island of Patmos for preaching the word of God and speaking about Jesus. *10*It was the Lord's Day, and I was worshiping in the Spirit. Suddenly, I heard a loud voice behind me, a voice that sounded like a trumpet blast. *11*It said, "Write down what you see, and send it to the seven churches: Ephesus, Smyrna, Pergamum, Thyatira, Sardis, Philadelphia, and Laodicea." *12*When I turned to see who was speaking to me, I saw seven gold lampstands. *13*And standing in the middle of the lampstands was the Son of Man. He was wearing a long robe with a gold sash across his chest. _14_His head and his hair were white like wool, as white as snow. And his eyes were bright like flames of fire. _15_His feet were as bright as bronze refined in a furnace, and his voice thundered like mighty ocean waves. _16_He held seven stars in his right hand, and a sharp two-edged sword came from his mouth. And his face was as bright as the sun in all its brilliance. _17_When I saw him, I fell at his feet as dead. But he laid his right hand on me and said, "Don't be afraid! I am the First and the Last. _18_I am the living one who died. Look, I am alive forever and ever! And I hold the keys of death and the grave. _19_Write down what you have seen—both the things that are now happening and the things that will happen later. _20_This is the meaning of the seven stars you saw in my right hand and the seven gold lampstands: The seven stars are the angels of the seven churches, and the seven lampstands are the seven churches.

Explained in a nutshell!

You've always heard about 'the end of the world', haven't you? Did you ever wonder if there was one, what happened after that? The *Revelation* is all about Jesus Christ and the future events in our world leading up to His Second Coming to Earth. He appears to John who is in prayer on the Island of Patmos. John gets a peek into Heaven. He sees the *glorified* Jesus—not merely the man who walked the land of Israel and was crucified 2000 years ago. This sight of the glorified Son of God caused John to faint! Jesus comforted John and promised a blessing to anyone who studies and takes to heart the message of *Revelation*. John is then told to pass *Revelation* around to seven particular churches in Asia. It's the same book left to us to study today!

Key verses: 1:5, 18

Key word: Jesus Christ

Focus locus—themes and threads throughout!

- **The Resurrection of Jesus**—Resurrection means *to stand again*. Jesus rose from the dead to show that He had power over our worst fear—death! (See chapter 11, and Acts 2:24.)

- **The Second Coming of Jesus**—This is what *Revelation* is all about. Jesus came to earth the first time as a baby in Bethlehem. His mission was to grow up as God in human flesh and die for our sins. When He returns, He'll come as a mighty king and punish sin on earth. *Revelation* tells the story of the events leading up to this! (See Jude 14 and chapters 12 and 19.)

- **Death**—Death is unnatural. Death entered the human race when Adam and Eve disobeyed God in the Garden of Eden. Later, their son (Cain) killed his brother (Abel). People have died ever since. Though your body will die, your soul and spirit—the *real* you—lives forever. God did not plan for your body to die. Since God has power over all things—even death—He'll resurrect (raise up) our bodies from the graves someday, and death will be defeated. *Death* will die! (See Rom. 5:12, and chapter 14.)

- **Angels**—Angels are God's messengers. They can look like us, but they never die. Angels aren't the spirits of dead Christians. We don't become angels when we die! Angels don't marry or have children, and most of them don't have wings! There are a set number of angels, which never changes. Some angels are more powerful than others, and they can sometimes look very frightening to us when they appear! Angels help do God's work on earth, are very curious about your salvation (I Pet. 1:12), and are not to be worshipped (Rev. 22:8-9).

Getting to know Jesus!

- *Jesus Christ*—'Jesus' means *savior*, and 'Christ' speaks of Him as God's Chosen One. *Revelation* is the 'revealing' of God's Son as Savior of all who call upon Him.

- *The One who is, always was, and is still to come (the Living One who died, and is alive forever and ever)*—This describes Jesus as timeless, or what we call *eternal*. Jesus was before time, exists in time, and will exist after time is no more. Jesus created time. Jesus was born as a human baby 2000 years ago in Bethlehem to grow up and die for our sins. He was crucified on a Roman cross, but three days later He came back from the dead to show his power over death. Jesus is eternal. He'll never die again. (See Phil. 2:9-10.)

- *The Faithful Witness*—Here you see Jesus as the One who was faithful and obedient to His Father's will in all things—even unto death. Faithful also means that everything Jesus said was the real deal—the absolute truth. The word 'witness' can mean one who gives up their life—all the way to death if necessary—for their beliefs. Jesus was faithful to God all the way to death. (See chapter 3.)

- *The Almighty*—This describes God's awesome power as The Creator! It's strength in action. His power is irresistible! *The Lord God Almighty* describes God as awesome—almost frighteningly powerful!

- *The 'I am'*—This describes Christ's *timelessness*. Though we can't understand this, Jesus always was, and always will be. He is outside of time, and isn't controlled by it. He controls time!

- *The Alpha & Omega/the Beginning and the End/the First and the Last*— This shows Jesus as the beginning and ending of all things. He was before all things and will always exist! (Col. 1:15-20; Ps. 90)

- *Lord*—Lord means master. A master is someone you serve.

- *The Son of Man*—This was the favorite title of Jesus for Himself. It describes Him in His humanity when He was born into the world at Bethlehem. (Matt. 8:20)

- *The first to rise from the dead*—This speaks of Jesus as the first one to come back from the dead and not die again. While others in Scripture were raised from the dead, they finally died. Not so Jesus! He defeated death! (See I Cor. 15:20; Col. 1:13-18.)

- *The Commander of the rulers of the world*—Here is Jesus as the Heavenly general who will lead the armies of Heaven to the earth at His Second Coming! He is greater than any mighty warrior who ever lived!

- *He that loved us and freed us from our sins*—What a beautiful description of Jesus! Because He loved you so much, He died to forgive all your sins!

Nuts to crack—terms to know!

- **Revelation**—This means to *unwrap* or to *reveal*. *Revelation* isn't meant to be hidden! *Revelation* is meant to be studied so that you might see the real Jesus in all His power and glory! God wants you to know what's going to happen because Jesus is coming soon! God also wants you to remember that everything was made by, for, and through His Son Jesus!

- **John**—John was one of Jesus' closest and youngest followers (disciples). But when he wrote *Revelation,* John was an old man. Maybe because he'd been so close to Jesus, he was the one Jesus chose to write about the Second Coming! (See John 13:23; 20:2-8.)

- **Testimony**—This means to speak about something you see, hear, or know. It can also mean *witness.* You give your testimony as a witness in court. When you tell others about Christ, you're giving testimony to what you know Christ has done in your life. Sometimes this word can mean 'martyr'—to die for your beliefs. (See chapters 2 and 3.)

- **Blessing**—There's a special blessing on you for studying and obeying the messages of *Revelation*! This blessing isn't promised for most of the other books of the Bible! Only God knows what the special blessing will be, but expect it! *Revelation* is a very special book!

- **Prophecy**—This means to speak about the future. The Book of *Revelation* is a book of prophecy. Many of the people in the Old Testament spoke about Jesus' first coming. John got to write about His Second Coming! Studying prophecy is *very* important. (See I Cor. 4:5; II Tim. 4:1-2.)

- **Seven Churches**—A church isn't just the building we worship in, but also refers to all genuine Christians from all time periods since Jesus was on earth. That body of Christians is called God's *church.* Here, though, it does mean seven specific churches in Asia when John was writing *Revelation.* He wanted them to read and understand about the end of time and the Second Coming of Jesus. Those seven churches had the same problems you and I have today. What God told them, He's telling you too.

- **Grace & Peace**—Grace means to receive some wonderful gift you definitely don't deserve. Peace is that wonderfully satisfied feeling you have when you get that gift. God gave you forgiveness for all your sins. That gift cost God the life of His Son. (See chapter 14.)

- **Sevenfold Spirit**—There are creatures in Heaven beyond our ability to imagine! These seven spirits are mysterious. We only need to know that they are holy, are blazing in appearance, serve God, and have a purpose in Heaven! (See chapter 4, and Isa. 11:2)

- **They which pierced Him**—This probably means the Jews, who had Jesus crucified. (See John 19:37; Zech. 12:10.)

- **Amen**—Amen means *let it be*, or *so be it*. (See chapter 3.)

- **Tribulation (Great Tribulation)**—A seven-year time of great trouble that will come upon the world just before Jesus returns. This period is described in *Revelation*, and will involve Israel, Antichrist, and earth-shaking natural disasters worse than have ever happened before. (See chapter 6.)

- **Kingdom**—God's kingdom is when Jesus rules on earth, and sin isn't able to make people act wickedly. God certainly doesn't have His kingdom on earth today, but someday He will. We'll get to that later in chapter 20!

- **Patmos**—Patmos is an island in the Mediterranean Sea. The Romans exiled John to this island for preaching about Jesus.

- **In the Spirit**—John had probably been in prayer when God gave him *Revelation*. (See 4:2; 17:3; 21:10.)

- **Lord's Day**—This was either Sunday, or it meant that John was in the spirit of deep prayer.

- **Seven lampstands**—Lampstands were large candleholders. Their purpose was to shed light on everything around them. Jesus is also seen as such a light (John 9:4-5).

- **Seven Stars**—In this passage, stars probably mean the ministers or guardian angels of the seven particular churches in John's day to which this book was written. If these churches had guardian angels, do you think you might have them too?

- **Sharp sword**—A sword cuts. A sharp sword can cut a very fine line. Jesus is the Sharp Sword that can cut between good and evil, our actions and our intentions. Jesus is the final Judge of all things. He is the Word of God. He'll make no mistakes. (See chapter 19, and Heb. 4:12; Eph. 6:17.)

- **Keys of Hell and death**—Keys are always symbols of authority or ownership. To have the keys to something means you control it. As the Creator, Jesus has power over everything—even over the power of death. Jesus defeated death through his resurrection! As bad as things get in *Revelation*, remember, Jesus is in control. He has the keys to not just life, but death and the next world, too! (See John 1:1-3.)

- **Mystery**—We all love a mystery! A mystery is a story that takes figuring out! Even though God knows everything about the past and future, we don't. To us, the future is a mystery, which God reveals to us over time. Can you find the eight *mysteries* listed in the Bible?

Backpack for the road—Principles to Ponder!

- *God wants us to know the future!*—*Revelation* tells us about Jesus in His power and glory. *Revelation* is meant to be read and studied—not hidden! God doesn't want to us to be surprised or afraid when we see *Revelation's* events begin. These lead to the Second Coming of Jesus!

- *God alone is Creator!*—God made everything. Everything belongs to Him. Everything was made by Him, for Him, and to glorify Him! (See Col. 1:15-17.)

- *God is sovereign—even over death!*—Sovereign means that God has all power over all things. Sometimes God lets bad things happen so that He can overcome them for a greater good. He even lets people die. Remember this when He lets hurtful things happen in your life. (See chapters 3 & 6, and Rom. 8:28.)

- *Lampstand Lesson*—A candle (lampstand) burns brighter when the wax and crud is scraped away from its wick. God wants your life to be a bright shining light in the world. Why? Because sin has brought spiritual darkness to God's world. Christians are called the 'light' of the world because it's our job to tell the world about the salvation from sins that Jesus provided. But this light must burn brightly! Sometimes God allows troubles and hardships in your life to scrape away the crud. God is watching you and 'trimming' your wicks! Don't let the sinful temptations of the world dull your Christian witness. Trim your own wicks so God doesn't have to! (See Heb. 12:6.)

Journal for the journey—My reflections!

- ✓ Is Jesus *my* Lord and Savior? Do I look *forward* to the Second Coming of Christ?

- ✓ Do I need to study my Bible more? Do I have a set study time?

- ✓ When bad happens, do I trust God that He has a *purpose*?

- ✓ Have *I* ever suffered for my faith?

- ✓ Do I understand that Jesus *made* me, *keeps* me, and is *in charge of* my life even when it stinks?

- ✓ How do *I* worship in the Spirit?

- ✓ Do I have 'wicks' in my life that I need to trim, such as things I *say* or *do*?

- ✓ Am I a *light* to my non-Christian friends? Do I show them Jesus?

- ✓ Do I speak only things that are *honest* and *true*?

- ✓ Could I *die* for my Christianity?

- ✓ Has God ever spoken to me when I prayed? How did I know? If He hasn't, why not?

- ✓ What would I say to Jesus if He appeared to me right now? What might He say to *me*?

- ✓ Grace was the wonderful gift you received when you became a Christian. How do you feel about such a precious gift?

- ✓ What can I learn from the fact that Jesus stands in the *middle* of His churches? (See Matt. 18:20.)

- ✓ How can I become a 'star' according to God? (See Dan. 12:3!)

Chapter 2

"Seven Emails from Jesus—Part 1"
(*Trouble*: don't give up! *Temptation*: don't give in!)

1 "Write this letter to the angel of the church in Ephesus. This is the message from the one who holds the seven stars in his right hand, the one who walks among the seven gold lampstands: *2* "I know all the things you do. I have seen your hard work and your patient endurance. I know you don't tolerate evil people. You have examined the claims of those who say they are apostles but are not. You have discovered they are liars. *3* You have patiently suffered for me without quitting. *4* But I have this complaint against you. You don't love me or each other as you did at first! *5* Look how far you have fallen from your first love! Turn back to me again and work as you did at first. If you don't, I will come and remove your lampstand from its place among the churches. *6* But there is this about you that is good: You hate the deeds of the immoral Nicolaitans, just as I do. *7* "Anyone who is willing to hear should listen to the Spirit and understand what the Spirit is saying to the churches. Everyone who is victorious will eat from the tree of life in the paradise of God. *8* "Write this letter to the angel of the church in Smyrna. This is the message from the one who is the First and the Last, who died and is alive: *9* "I know about your suffering and your poverty—but you're rich! I know the slander of those opposing you. They say they are Jews, but they really aren't because theirs is a synagogue of Satan. *10* Don't be afraid of what you're about to suffer. The Devil will throw some of you into prison and put you to the test. You'll be persecuted for 'ten days.' Remain faithful even when facing death, and I will give you the crown of life. *11* "Anyone who is willing to hear should listen to the Spirit and understand what the Spirit is saying to the churches. Whoever is victorious won't be hurt by the second death. *12* "Write this letter to the angel of the church in Pergamum. This is the message from the one who has a sharp two-edged sword: *13* "I know that you live in the city where that great throne of Satan is located, and yet you have remained loyal to me. And you refused to deny me even when Antipas, my faithful witness, was martyred among you by Satan's followers. *14* And yet I have a few complaints against you. You tolerate some among you who are like Balaam, who showed Balak how to trip up the people of Israel. He taught them to worship idols by eating food offered to idols and by committing sexual sin. *15* In the same way, you have some Nicolaitans among you—people who follow the same teaching and commit the same sins. *16* Repent, or I will come to you suddenly and fight against them with the sword of my mouth. *17* "Anyone who is willing to hear should listen to the Spirit and understand what the Spirit is saying to the churches. Everyone who is victorious will eat of the manna that has been hidden away in Heaven. And I will give to each one a white stone, and on the stone will be engraved a new name that no one knows except the one who receives it. *18* "Write this letter to the angel of the church in Thyatira. This is the message from the Son of God, whose eyes are bright like flames of fire, whose feet are like polished bronze: *19* "I know all the things you do—your love, your faith, your service, and your patient endurance. And I can see your constant improvement in all these things. *20* But I have this complaint against you. You're permitting that woman—that Jezebel who calls herself a prophet—to lead my servants astray. She is encouraging them to worship idols, eat food offered to idols, and commit sexual sin. *21* I gave her time to repent, but she would not turn away from her immorality. *22* Therefore, I will throw her upon a sickbed, and she'll suffer greatly with all who commit adultery with her, unless they turn away from all their evil deeds. *23* I will strike her children dead. And all the churches will know that I am the one who searches out the thoughts and intentions of every person. And I will give to each of you whatever you deserve. *24* But I also have a message for the rest of you in Thyatira who have not followed this false teaching ('deeper truths,' as they call them—depths of Satan, really). I will ask nothing more of you *25* except that you hold tightly to what you have until I come. *26* "To all who are victorious, who obey me to the very end, I will give authority over all the nations. *27* They will rule the nations with an iron rod and smash them like clay pots. *28* They will have the same authority I received from my Father, and I will also give them the morning star! *29* Anyone who is willing to hear should listen to the Spirit and understand what the Spirit is saying to the churches.

Explained in a nutshell!

Jesus is carefully watching everything you and I do. He loves us and wants us to grow in our Christian faith. But sometimes, growth is painful. Because He's like a good parent, sometimes He has to discipline us. Sometimes—for our own good—we have to hear what we may not enjoy hearing. The messages to the first three churches both encourage and warn them. These messages are for you and me too. To Ephesus, Jesus compliments their hard work for Him and their hatred of evil. But He warns them that their dedication is starting to fade, and they're in danger of losing the great Heavenly rewards He has for them. To Smyrna, Jesus reminds them that even though they're poor by the world's standards, they are rich by His. Jesus reminds them what He would remind you—not everyone may be as 'Christian' as they look. The devil is a pro at deception, but God is more powerful than Satan. God is in charge! Stand for your faith—there's a Heavenly reward for you someday! To Pergamum, Jesus says He understands they live in bad company. But they're told not to give in to temptations of sexual sins! While some Christians died for their Christianity, others began to tolerate—and even join—the evildoers. 'Repent and change your ways!' Jesus warns them. He won't put up with sin even from His children. To Thyatira, Jesus compliments their growth in Christianity, but also warns against tolerating false religions. Even religion is sinful to God when it's the wrong religion. God will punish every type of sinfulness, even the sin of false religion. Jesus urges them to be faithful so that they will rule with Him someday!

Key verse: 2:5

Key word: Repent

Focus locus—themes and threads throughout!

- **Crowns/Rewards**—Crowns in the Bible can be either kingly authority or Heavenly rewards. Crowns are seen as both in *Revelation*. God will reward you for the good things you do for Him as a Christian. While these good things don't make you a Christian—only God can save you from your sins—they're evidence you *are* a Christian. God never forgets the things you do or say to bring Him glory. Someday, God will reward you! (See chapter 14, I Cor.9:24; I Thes. 2:19-20; I Pet. 5:1-4; II Tim. 4:8 and Jam. 1:12.)

- **Staying faithful to God!**—There are many religions that claim to be able to lead you to God. Islam, Mormonism, Hinduism, and Scientology are just a few. Some religions say there are many gods or no God at all. The Bible is God's instruction manual for life. Read and study it to know the truth about life and death God wants you to know! Jesus said He was the one and only way to Heaven—stay faithful to His Word! (See Matt. 24:13.) This is the only way to be *'victorious'* in God's eyes!

- **Remaining pure in a sinful world!**—There are many things in this world that pull you away from God. Temptations such as sex outside of marriage, lying, stealing, and many other things can ruin your Christian witness to others. Don't ruin yours. Put pleasing God first in your life. (See chapters 3, 14 & 18, and I John 2:15.)

Getting to know Jesus!

- *He who holds the Seven Stars*—(see chapter 1)

- *He who walks among the Seven Lampstands*—  Jesus is always watching His children. We saw earlier that these lampstands (or candlesticks) refer to churches. When you're a Christian, Jesus is never far from you. Jesus wants to keep you filled with the oil of His Spirit!

- *The Wick trimmer*—Sometimes God allows things in your life to scrape away the crud. God is watching you and 'trimming' your wicks! Don't let the sinful temptations of the world dull your Christian witness. Trim your own wicks so God doesn't have to! (See chapter 1 and John 15:1-2.)

- *The Resurrection & the life*—(see chapters 1 & 11)

- *The First & the Last*—As in chapter one (see Alpha & Omega) Jesus is the beginning and the ending of all things. He created everything, and everything (including you!) exists for his glory (Matt. 28:20).

- *He that was dead but is alive*—(see chapter 1)

- *The Sharp Sword*—(see chapter 1)

- *The Son of God*—This is Jesus' most glorious title! He is both God and the Son of God. How Jesus could be both God and God's Son is a mystery. We can't totally understand this. Basically, Jesus was always one with God, but when He came to earth to die for our sins 2000 years ago, becoming human, He did God's will. Jesus learned as a son learns from a parent. He was always God in spirit, but He learned obedience as the Son of God.

- *He with eyes of fire and feet of bronze*—This is a very strange picture of Jesus! His 'fiery eyes' mean that He sees, knows, and understands everything! In the Bible bronze stands for judgment. The gentle Jesus born a baby in Bethlehem 2000 years ago will come to earth the second time as the mighty Judge who knows every person's heart. The first time, He came to save. The Second Coming will be to judge! Aren't you glad your sins are forgiven? Are you looking forward to Christ's return?

- *He who searches the minds and hearts*— Because Jesus is God He knows everything about everyone. (Compare 22:16; Heb. 4:13, 10:13; Psalms 11:4; 139.)

- *The Morning Star*—What a beautiful picture of Jesus this is! Have you ever seen the last bright star in the sky just before sunrise in the morning? That's not a star—it's the planet Venus. Only those who are looking for it see the morning star. As the morning star, Jesus reminds us that He should be the first thing we think of each day of our life. Also, it seems to suddenly appear in the sky—this is how Jesus will come someday! (See II Pet. 1:19 and chapter 22.)

Nuts to crack—terms to know!

- **Angels**—(see chapter 1)

- **Church**—(see chapter 1)

- **Ephesus**—Like all 7 of these churches, Ephesus was in what is now Turkey. Another Bible book (Ephesians) was also written to that city. (See Acts 18:18-26; 20:26-38; 19:23-41.)

- **Apostle**—An apostle means *one who is sent out to deliver a message.* The original Apostles were men who followed Jesus and went out across their world to spread His good news (gospel) about forgiveness of sins.

- **First love**—Your first love doesn't refer to your first crush, or your first date. Your first love is the most important love in your life. It's the love of your highest priority. Your first love should be for Jesus Christ. He died for your sins so that you could spend forever with Him in Heaven someday. What do you put ahead of Jesus on your 'most loved' list? (See Eph. 3:17-19; Mark 12:28-34; I John 5:1-3; John 15:10; I Cor. 13:1-13.)

- **Repentance**—Repentance means to change your mind. When you change your desire for the things of the world to a desire for the things of God, you repent. When you tell God you're genuinely sorry for your sins, this is repentance. When we truly repent, God forgives us. (See Matt. 9:13 and chapters 3 & 16.)

- **The Nicolaitans**—No one really knows for sure who these people were. Their name means *to boss over the people*, so maybe that's what they did.

- **Having an ear to hear**—This mysterious phrase tells us to make sure we understand what was just said. It means: 'Did you *really* get what I just said?' It stresses the importance of the message. *Revelation* is meant to be understood, but it takes patience and prayer. (Compare 2:11, 29; 3:6, 13, 22; 13:9.)

- **Spirit—God's Holy Spirit**—This isn't some ghost, but the very presence of God, which lives inside your heart if you're a Christian! God's Spirit is even more effective than your conscience at telling you right from wrong. Has God's Spirit spoken to you lately? (See John 14:16-17; 16:7-15; Eph. 1:13-14.)

- **Tree of Life**—This tree was in the Garden of Eden. It was the tree whose fruit brought enduring life. When Adam and Eve sinned, God forced them out of the garden, and barred the way to the Tree of Life. God will restore this tree to us some-day. (See Gen. 3:22 and chapter 22.)

- **Paradise of God**—Paradise means *beautiful garden*. The Garden of Eden was God's paradise where He put Adam and Eve to enjoy His creation. Since the Garden of Eden is gone, this paradise probably means Heaven.

- **Smyrna**—Like all 7 of these churches, Smyrna was in what is now Turkey. This poor church suffered for their faith. The name 'Smyrna' comes from the word 'myrrh'—a spice taken from a thorny tree, and related to death and suffering! (See Matt. 2:11; John 19:39.)

- **Blaspheme**—(see chapters 13 & 16)

- **Synagogue**—A synagogue is a Jewish place of worship.

- **Satan/the devil**—The devil is an angel. He was one of the most power-ful angels God ever created. (Yes, God created everything!) This angel was once beautiful and wise. Then, along with other angels, the devil rebelled against God and became terribly wicked. God allows the devil limited access to Heaven. Now, Satan desires to bring evil to our world, and cause humans to be evil, too. Satan's future is Hell (chapter 20), which was made for him, but today Satan is very powerful in our world! (See chapters 12 & 13 and Isa. 14:12-17; Ezek. 28; I Peter 5:8; Matt. 9:34; 13:19; John 8:44; Eph. 4:27.)

- **Tribulation ten days**—While tribulation means *trouble,* we can't know for sure what this phrase meant to the people who read it in John's day. It was probably a local persecution by the Romans. For certain—they knew the meaning. This isn't the Great Tribulation (chapter 6).

- **The second death**—You know what death is. Death is when your soul and spirit are separated from your body. The 'second death' is when your soul and spirit are *forever* separated from God. It is Hell. It is forever. It's the destiny of every person who has not given his or her life to God through Jesus. (See Matt. 10:28 and chapters 9, 14, 17, 19 & 20.)

- **Pergamum**—Like all seven of these churches, Pergamum was in what is now Turkey. In John's day, Pergamum was one of Asia's great cities.

- **Satan's throne**—The devil must have had quite an influence in the church at Pergamum! Maybe this was the great statue of Zeus that once was there.

- **Antipas**—He was someone the early readers knew. Exactly who Antipas was is lost to us—but not to God. None of us are ever forgotten by God.

- **Martyr**—A martyr also means a witness (see chapter 1). A martyr is someone who dies for their belief and trust in God. Do you love God enough to die for Him? (See chapters 1 & 3, and John 15:21; 21:18-19.)

- **Balaam**—Balaam was a man in the Old Testament who caused people to leave their worship of the true God. God doesn't look kindly on *anyone* who might try to lead you away from Jesus! (See Num. 22-25.)

- **Sacrificing to idols**—Whenever we give our obedience and love to anything other than the true God, we sacrifice ourselves and our time to *idols*. Idols can be statues, cars, money, sexual pleasures, etc. Do you have any *idols*? Is there anything you love more than God?

- **Fornication**—This is sex outside of marriage. (See chapter 14.)

- **Manna**—Manna is Heavenly food. It was the special flakes of white sweet food that God dropped from Heaven for the Hebrews to eat when they left Egypt (Ex. 16:11,32).

- **The white stone**—Ancient people sometimes voted whether a person was guilty or innocent by the color of stones. A white stone meant innocent, a black stone—guilty. It was also sometimes used as an admission ticket to events. Can you find the 5 *white* items in *Revelation*?

- **New name**—Names were extremely important in Bible times! Your name usually reflected every hope your parents had for you. Even the name 'Jesus' means 'savior'! What does your name mean? Can you find the 6 *new* things in *Revelation*? (See chapters 3 & 19.)

- **Thyatira**—Like all 7 of these churches, Thyatira was in what is now Turkey. This city was famous for sacrificing animals to the gods. It was the city of 'religion'.

- **Jezebel**—Jezebel was a very wicked queen in Israel who made her own people worship false gods. The reference here is to the worship of gods and idols that have nothing to do with the real God! (I Kings 9:30; 16:29-33; 19:1-3; 21:1-16; II Kings 9:22.)

- **Adultery**—In a marriage, adultery is when one person is unfaithful to the other. Adultery here means that someone is unfaithful to the God they claim to worship. God hates unfaithfulness! Is there something in this world that could draw your faithfulness away from your God? If so—*that* becomes your god!

- **Great tribulation**—(see chapter 6)

- **Depths of Satan**—No one knows what this was, but people in John's day knew.

- **Rod of iron**—Rulers often carried rods. Rods stood for power, sort of like a whipping stick. When Jesus returns to rule on earth, He won't rule like a wimp. He'll rule with a firm hand and a rod of iron. He won't let sin take over the world as it has today under earthly rulers. (See Ps. 2:9 and chapter 19.)

Backpack for the road—Principles to Ponder!

- *No work we do for God is lost or forgotten!*—God will never forget even one single thing you do for His glory. When you witness for Jesus, show kindness to others, forgive those who don't deserve it, study your Bible—everything is remembered by God. Someday you'll be rewarded for these things, even things you don't even recall doing. God never forgets! (See chapter 2, and *Great White Throne* in chapter 20.)

- *Tolerance has its limits!*—Our world tells us we must be tolerant of others. Up to a point, this is true. But God doesn't tolerate sin, and neither should you. Like God, you should call sin what it is—evil. If you tolerate sin, you show you agree with it, and if you call yourself a Christian this is wrong. Don't be led astray by cults, religions, or other people who try to lead you away from the things of God! (See II Cor. 6:14-7:1; II Tim. 2:19-22.)

- *When things get tough—hang on—even when it's hard to!*—God never promised you that being a Christian would be easy. In fact, He said it would be hard. Don't give up or give in when things get tough! Let hard times make you stronger! Run the race of life with patience and courage (Heb. 6:12; James 1:3-4; 5:10-11; I Cor. 6:2; II Cor. 4:17; I John 5:4-5).

- *Don't lose your Christian witness by 'soiling' your garments with sin!*—The world is watching you. Calling yourself a Christian makes others keep an eye on what you do and what you say. (See Eph. 1:4; I Peter 1:15-16; II Peter 3:11-14.)

- *More light means more responsibility—and greater judgment!*—Do you know right from wrong? Then you're responsible for doing right. God's standard of judgment is that if you know to do right and don't, your punishment will be greater than if you don't know right from wrong (Luke 12:48).

- *Don't cause your 'weaker' Christian brother to sin!*—As a Christian, God has set you free to live in Christ. Some things are *clearly* wrong, such as stealing and murder. But other things are questionable, such as what day you worship on, or whether you eat meat or are a vegetarian. Although you're free to follow your conscience, you shouldn't force your beliefs on other Christians. Remember, in questionable things, they're free, *too* (I Cor. 8:7; 10:20).

- *Persecution for being a Christian WILL come—get used to it!*—Do non-Christians make fun of your dedication to Christ? Are you teased for your faith? Hey, this is a good sign! God says that this proves you're His child! Hang in there! They persecuted Jesus and his followers. Do you really think they'll do *less* to you? (See chapters 3 & 6, and II Tim. 1:7-8; 3:12; Heb. 2:10; 4:15; 5:8; I Pet. 1:6-7; 2:20-21; John 16:33; Rom. 8:28-31.)

- *There are a lot of 'pretend' Christians in the world—be careful!*—Not everyone who calls themselves a Christian *is* one. Some people call themselves Christian when it's convenient, but they really haven't turned over their life to Christ. Just don't be surprised when those who call themselves a Christian don't act like one. You'll find out whether they're the 'real thing' over time, and when real trouble comes! (See chapters 3, 13, 17; II Cor. 11:1-4; I John 4:1-6; II John 7-11.)

- *Never give in to the temptation to compromise with what's wrong!*—Compromise means to make a deal. The devil would love to make a deal with you! His offer in trying to get you to sin sounds like some of these: 'Once can't hurt', or 'everybody's doing it'. Don't give in! (See II John 10; Rom. 16:17; II Thes. 3:6.)

- *Those sins you think are 'secret' aren't—God knows!*—Did you ever think you could 'sneak in' a sin or two that God would miss? Think again! God knows everything you do, and every word you speak. He even knows the intentions of your heart. Don't ever think you can fool God! (See Prov. 9:17-18; Luke 8:17.)

- *Be careful of those who have 'secret insight' into God's Word!*—Whenever others claim to have knowledge of God and His will that doesn't square with the Bible, run for your life! Of course, this assumes you *know* what the Bible tells us is right and wrong! It's very important to study God's Word, and just as important to know when others are trying to *add to* or *subtract from* it! (See II Tim. 2:15; I John 4:1-3; I Cor. 8:7; 10:20; II Cor. 11:14; Prov. 14:12.)

- *You'll reap what you sow—what goes around comes around!*—Nature has a law: you only grow what you plant. Tomato seeds don't grow onions. Plant in life only what you want to grow. Kindness, honesty, and forgiveness are good seeds. Cheating, gossip and lying are not. What you plant, grows. But not overnight. When you plant good seeds in life—or bad ones—remember, growth takes time. What doesn't grow tomorrow will start to sprout eventually. It's a law of nature. It's also a law of God! (See chapter 16 and Gal. 6:7; Matt. 7:2; Hosea 8:7.)

Journal for the journey—My reflections and prayer

- ✓ Is there anything I need to repent for? Am I hiding any secret sins?

- ✓ Since Jesus is always watching me, is there anything He might see that would displease Him? What might He say to me that I really wouldn't want to hear?

- ✓ What thoughts live in my mind that it worries me Jesus knows about?

- ✓ Are there any sinful temptations in my life that I'm thinking about *giving in* to?

- ✓ Do I tolerate sins in others by laughing at dirty jokes, gossip, or sexual references?

- ✓ Is there something that's tempting me to compromise my Christian beliefs?

- ✓ Does my *fire of love* for godly things still burn brightly? Am I a light to the world?

- ✓ Am I tempted to experience other religions such as Scientology, Islam, Hinduism, etc., or read about the cults?

- ✓ Am I watching each day for the Second Coming of Jesus?

- ✓ Am I studying my Bible each day as I should?

- ✓ Do I have an *ear to hear* what God says to me through His Word?

- ✓ Am I running the race of life with trust and courage when the tough times come?

- ✓ Do bad times shake my trust in God?

- ✓ Would I be willing to die for my Christian beliefs?

- ✓ Are there any things in my life I'm putting ahead of God?

- ✓ Would anyone want to become a Christian—or want to know what a Christian is—by simply by watching my life?

- ✓ How can someone be *poor* in the world, and yet *rich* toward God?

- ✓ Am I keeping my body pure?

✓ Am I doing anything that might cause weaker Christians to *stumble* in their Christian walk?

✓ Do I sometimes stay quiet about Christian things because I'm afraid speaking up might make others hassle me?

✓ What *seeds* am I planting in my life?

✓ What rewards or crowns do I hope to have in Heaven someday?

✓ What *new name* would I like to be given by Jesus someday?

✓ Do I talk like most teens, or do I speak as if Jesus was right beside me? Remember, He is! (Col.2:18; 1Cor.9:27; Matt.24:13)

Chapter 3

"Seven Emails from Jesus—Part 2"
(Hold on: trust God, not yourself!)

_1_ "Write this letter to the angel of the church in Sardis. This is the message from the one who has the sevenfold Spirit of God and the seven stars: "I know all the things you do, and that you have a reputation for being alive—but you're dead. _2_ Now wake up! Strengthen what little remains, for even what is left is at the point of death. Your deeds are far from right in the sight of God. _3_ Go back to what you heard and believed at first; hold to it firmly and turn to me again. Unless you do, I will come upon you suddenly, as unexpected as a thief. _4_ "Yet even in Sardis there are some who have not soiled their garments with evil deeds. They will walk with me in white, for they are worthy. _5_ All who are victorious will be clothed in white. I will never erase their names from the Book of Life, but I will announce before my Father and his angels that they are mine. _6_ Anyone who is willing to hear should listen to the Spirit and understand what the Spirit is saying to the churches. _7_ "Write this letter to the angel of the church in Philadelphia. This is the message from the one who is holy and true. He is the one who has the key of David. He opens doors, and no one can shut them; he shuts doors, and no one can open them. _8_ "I know all the things you do, and I have opened a door for you that no one can shut. You have little strength, yet you obeyed my word and did not deny me. _9_ Look! I will force those who belong to Satan—those liars who say they are Jews but are not—to come and bow down at your feet. They will acknowledge that you're the ones I love. _10_ "Because you have obeyed my command to persevere, I will protect you from the great time of testing that will come upon the whole world to test those who belong to this world. _11_ Look, I am coming quickly. Hold on to what you have, so that no one will take away your crown. _12_ All who are victorious will become pillars in the Temple of my God, and they will never have to leave it. And I will write my God's name on them, and they will be citizens in the city of my God—the new Jerusalem that comes down from Heaven from my God. And they will have my new name inscribed upon them. _13_ Anyone who is willing to hear should listen to the Spirit and understand what the Spirit is saying to the churches. _14_ "Write this letter to the angel of the church in Laodicea. This is the message from the one who is the Amen—the faithful and true witness, the ruler of God's creation: _15_ "I know all the things you do, that you're neither hot nor cold. I wish you were one or the other! _16_ But since you're like lukewarm water, I will spit you out of my mouth! _17_ You say, 'I am rich. I have everything I want. I don't need a thing!' And you don't realize that you're wretched and miserable and poor and blind and naked. _18_ I advise you to buy gold from me—gold that has been purified by fire. Then you'll be rich. And also buy white garments so you'll not be shamed by your nakedness. And buy ointment for your eyes so you'll be able to see. _19_ I am the one who corrects and disciplines everyone I love. Be diligent and turn from your indifference. _20_ "Look! Here I stand at the door and knock. If you hear me calling and open the door, I will come in, and we will share a meal as friends. _21_ I will invite everyone who is victorious to sit with me on my throne, just as I was victorious and sat with my Father on his throne. _22_ Anyone who is willing to hear should listen to the Spirit and understand what the Spirit is saying to the churches."

Explained in a nutshell!

To Sardis, Jesus reminds them that He knows all things. These people look like real Christians, but they aren't. Jesus warns them that He'll judge such fakery—even in His own children. He'll publicly reward those real Christians someday—in front of Heaven and earth. To Philadelphia, Jesus compliments those standing up for Him—even though they have little influence among great people. To them, He'll give great opportunities, and they'll someday rule with Him over the mighty. He also reminds us that He's coming back sooner than we might think! To Laodicea, Jesus has nothing good to say. He tells them they think they're great and powerful, but not in God's eyes. Still, He gives them a chance to become great to God, but they have to deal with their attitude of too much pride.

Key verse: 3:10

Key word: door

Focus locus—themes and threads throughout!

- **The Open Door**—The Rapture—The word Rapture means *to snatch*. Many Christians believe that Jesus will suddenly snatch or Rapture them to Heaven before the terrible period called the Great Tribulation, which will come upon the earth in the future (see chapter 4 and Luke 21:36).

- **Failing to choose**—Everyone makes a choice of what they'll worship. Some people worship the things of this world, such as clothes, cars, or money. Others choose to worship false gods such as Buddha or Allah. As a Christian, you've chosen to worship the God of Abraham, Isaac, and Jacob. To choose to worship anything but the true God is to worship falsely. Even choosing to decide later is a choice. Be careful and deliberate in your choices. (Joshua 24:15)

- **God's discipline**—Discipline isn't always punishment. Like a loving parent, God disciplines His children. Not because He doesn't love them, but because He does! Never despise the discipline of those who love you. Discipline is like sandpaper. It feels rough and abrasive when it's in motion, but the final result is a smooth and polished surface. Discipline is for your good. (See Heb. 12:6-11 and chapters 4 & 8.)

- **God's justice**—God is holy. God punishes sin, since sin is the opposite of holiness. Because God is holy, He punishes sin. He wouldn't be holy if He didn't. When God judges sin—and our sinful world—don't think that He is unfair. God always does what's right—even when we don't fully understand Him. (See chapter 18, Nah.1:2-3, and II Thes.1:6-10.)

- **Keeping your focus on faithfulness!**—More and more, the pleasures of this world will pull you away from the things of God. Bible study, prayer, and worship sometimes get crowded out. While God put you in the world to enjoy it, never forget to keep focused on the things that matter most—the things you do for God! (See II Tim. 2:15.)

Getting to know Jesus!

- *He that has the Sevenfold Spirit of God & the Seven Stars of God*—(see chapter 1)

- *The one that is Holy & True*—Jesus is holy and trustworthy. He never sinned. He is the True God. Allah, Buddha, Mohammed—these are not God, neither can they save you from your sins. Jesus alone is God, and can save you! (See John 6:69; Acts 4:27.)

- *He that has the keys of David*—David was one of Israel's greatest kings. Jesus was born in the family line of David—the family of Judah—and inherited the right to reign as king. He has the key—the authority to be not only king of Israel, but King of Kings and Lord of Lords. He will be someday! (See Rev. 5:5 and 22:16; Isa. 22:22.)

- *The Amen*—In the TV show *Star Trek—the Next Generation*, Captain Picard would end his command with '*make it so!*' When we end our prayers, we say *amen* to sort of sum up or nail down our conversation with God. As the Amen, Jesus is the final 'summing up' of all God is and does. It is fixed, certain, and true. It is the label: 'for sure'! Jesus is God, and summed up all God is to us when He came to earth two thousand years ago. (See chapter 1.)

- *The Faithful & True Witness*—As we've already discussed, Jesus is the faithful and trustworthy representation of God. He never acted outside His Father's will. Jesus was also 'true', that is, the *genuine* Son of God. Jesus was also a *witness* for God since He came to the earth to reveal God's will, and die for our sins. It is His *death* that is key here, since 'witness' can also mean someone who dies for their beliefs. (See chapter 1.)

- *The Son of God*—see chapter 2.

- *The Ruler of Creation*—Jesus always existed. He was the First Creator of all things. (See chapter 1 and John 1:1-3.)

- *The Protector of His children*—A protector is someone who defends you—someone who looks out for you. Jesus is your Heavenly Protector. He defends you against every charge the devil might bring against you before God. Jesus not only saved you through His death, He also *keeps* you saved through His resurrection life! (See Matt.10:32 and Heb.7:25.)

- *The One knocking at your heart's door!*—Do you recall when you became a Christian? Did you feel a tugging on your heart calling you to make a decision? If so, this was the perfect picture of Jesus knocking at your heart's door. Just remember—*you* must open the door. Jesus never forces His way in. The door must be opened from the inside. (See John 1:11; Luke 8:8; 17:25.)

Nuts to crack—terms to know!

- **Angel**—(see chapter 1)

- **Sardis**—Like all 7 of these churches, Sardis was in what is now Turkey. Sardis was a once-wealthy city now living on past glory.

- **The Sevenfold Spirit**—(see chapter 1)

- **White garments**—Garments stand for how you live your life. White stands for purity and holiness. In other words, what the world sees when it looks at you. God wants your life to look clean and white to others. Make sure you don't do or say things that would soil the garment of your life. People are watching you.

- **The Book of Life**—We can't be sure about exactly what this book is, but it seems to be a special book where God records the names of all Christians. It is the book of eternal life. (See chapters 17 and 20.)

- **Church**—(see chapter 1)

- **Ears to hear**—(see chapter 2)

- **Philadelphia**—Like all 7 of these churches, Philadelphia was in what is now Turkey. This was the church of 'brotherly love', and lasted the longest of all the seven churches. Christ had nothing bad to say about these Christians!

- **The open door**—God pictures the way to salvation and Heaven as a door—open to any who would enter by accepting Jesus as Savior. Some see this door as the entrance into Heaven of all Christians before the time of great trouble ('tribulation'), which will someday come upon the earth. Through this door will instantly pass all the living Christians as well as the resurrected bodies of Christians who have died. This event is called the *Rapture*. The word *rapture* means *to snatch quickly*, and that's what God does here! (See I Cor. 12:4-6; 16:8-9; II Cor. 2:12; Col. 4:3.)

- **Great time of testing**—God tests His children the way gold is tested in a furnace! The great heat makes the gold more pure! Is God putting you through a test right now? If so, it's to make you a better Christian. If He's not testing you now, He will. Expect it!

- **Crowns**—(see chapter 2)

- **The importance of 'names'**—Names were very important in biblical days. Your name represented the real you. God will give you a special name someday. This name will represent your unique and special character to God! (See chapters 2 and 19.)

- **New Jerusalem**—(see chapter 21)

- **Laodicea**—Like all 7 of these churches, Laodicea was in what is now Turkey. Laodicea was a very wealthy—and very wicked—city. Christ had nothing good to say to these people.

- **Lukewarm water**—Lukewarm means neither hot nor cold. Have you ever tasted water that was lukewarm? It almost makes you sick. The point here is that God hates wishy-washy people who can't decide whether they want to follow Him or not. They make Him want to vomit! (See Josh. 24:15.)

- **Ointment for your eyes**—Laodicea was known for the medicine *"Tephra Phrygia"*, put on the eyes for healing. The point here is that people should wake up from their sinfulness and see the light of Christ. He is the only way to salvation.

- **Repent**—Means to be very sorry. (See chapters 2 & 16.)

- **Throne**—Where a king sits.

Backpack for the road—Principles to Ponder!

- *The easy life isn't necessarily the best life—God said we would suffer—* Get used to it, if you're a Christian, you're going to feel like you just don't 'fit in' sometimes. The world loves sin. As soon as you try to do right, the world will let you know you're different. Sometimes this will really hurt, but it's solid evidence you're a child of God! (See chapters 2 & 6 and John 16:33; I Thes. 3:2-4; James 1:3-5; I Peter 1:7.)

- *Looks can be deceiving—don't think everything is as it appears*—Not everything that looks good or Christian really is. Sometimes you see people who seem to *act* very Christian, but that's what it turns out to be—only an act. Don't believe everything is just as it appears. Even the devil can look like an angel of light! (See chapters 2, 12, 13, 16, 17 and II Cor. 11:14; I John 4:1-3; I Thes. 5:3; Prov. 14:12.)

- *Watch your Christian witness—slightly soiled means greatly reduced!*— As discussed above under white garments, you must be careful how you act and what you say. The world is watching you. When you speak or act wrongly, you hurt your chances of being an effective witness for Christ.

- *Stand for something, or you'll fall for anything!*—Stand up for what you believe. No one appreciates people who change their beliefs every time they change company. If you're going to call yourself a Christian—stand up for your Christianity. Don't try to please everyone. People will respect you if you stand up for your beliefs. (Josh. 24:15; I Kings 18:21; Matt. 24:12; Luke 24:32)

- *Keep in mind, whatever you do, Jesus is coming back!*—A good rule to remember when you're not sure whether something you want to do is right or wrong is this—ask yourself: 'Would I do this if Jesus were here?' *Wake up* from lazy Bible study! *Fill up* on His Word! *Get up* and go tell others! (See chapter 14 and I Cor. 10:13; Eph. 4:30; Matt. 24:43, 25:13; Luke 12:37; II Tim. 2:19; I Thes. 5:1-8.)

- *Be careful not to lose your reward when Jesus returns! Live clean!*—If you're a genuine Christian, you don't have to worry about losing your salvation. That was bought and paid for by the precious blood of Jesus. The rewards (crowns) you may earn, however, are a different story. God notes every good thing you have done for Him since you became a Christian. For these things, He'll reward you someday. But it's possible to lose such rewards by living sinfully. God has instructed you on what you should be doing as you wait for Christ to return! (See I John 2:28; II Tim. 1:8-16; 2:15; Rom. 1:16; Luke 9:26.)

- *Many hypocrites are out there—two-faced, and not what they appear!*— The word 'hypocrite' means someone who says one thing, but acts in a different way altogether. Have you noticed many people who wear the *WWJD* bracelets, but do and say wrong things? Do you 'walk your talk' as a Christian? Many people you'll meet talk a good Christian talk. They may even quote Scripture. But they're just wolves in sheep's clothing. Be genuine. Be real. Don't fall for smooth-talking so-called Christians who aren't what they appear. Anyone who uses the Bible to tell others right and wrong, but doesn't follow it him or herself is a hypocrite. Beware—they're out there. (See Matt. 6:2-16; 7:21-23; II Tim. 3:1-5.)

- *When God disciplines us, it's for our good, not punishment!*—Discipline is done in love; punishment may not be. Someone has said that God never spanks the devil's kids. Only His own. When God let's you go through tough times—and you know it's not because of sin—He may be just training you for greater things. Hard times are just God's sandpaper to smooth out your rough edges. Learn from God's discipline—it's not punishment! Don't feel that tough times are because God is far from you. It may be just the opposite. It may be that He's close enough—and caring enough—to iron out all your 'wrinkles' so that your life will appear beautiful to Him someday! Beware of the 'church of the easy life'! It won't be God's church! (See chapters 3 & 11, and I Cor. 4:17; Matt. 24:22; Prov. 3:12; Rom. 10:13; Heb. 12:6.)

Journal for the journey—My reflections!

- ✓ Do I sometimes find myself acting in a way to fit in with others? Am I compromising and being a hypocrite?

- ✓ Do I look for the lesson God and my parents are trying to teach me when tough times come? Do I realize such discipline only reflects their *love* for me?

- ✓ What is *my* reputation? Do my friends see me as I see myself? How does God see me?

- ✓ What part of my life that my friends see do I need to clean up?

- ✓ What door of opportunity has God opened up for me to do His will?

- ✓ What would I want to be doing when Jesus returns?

- ✓ What can I learn about 'brotherly love' from Rom. 12:10; I Thes. 4:9-10; Heb. 13:1; I Pet. 1:22, and II Peter 1:7?

- ✓ Which of the churches am I most like? *Why?*

Chapter 4

"First Snapshot of Heaven!"
(What's *really* going on up there?)

1 Then as I looked, I saw a door standing open in Heaven, and the same voice I had heard before spoke to me with the sound of a mighty trumpet blast. The voice said, "Come up here, and I will show you what must happen after these things." *2* And instantly I was in the Spirit, and I saw a throne in Heaven and someone sitting on it! *3* The one sitting on the throne was as brilliant as gemstones—jasper and carnelian. And the glow of an emerald circled his throne like a rainbow. *4* Twenty-four thrones surrounded him, and twenty-four elders sat on them. They were all clothed in white and had gold crowns on their heads. *5* And from the throne came flashes of lightning and the rumble of thunder. And in front of the throne were seven lampstands with burning flames. They are the seven spirits of God. *6* In front of the throne was a shiny sea of glass, sparkling like crystal. In the center and around the throne were four living beings, each covered with eyes, front and back. *7* The first of these living beings had the form of a lion; the second looked like an ox; the third had a human face; and the fourth had the form of an eagle with wings spread out as though in flight. *8* Each of these living beings had six wings, and their wings were covered with eyes, inside and out. Day after day and night after night they keep on saying, "Holy, holy, holy is the Lord God Almighty—the one who always was, who is, and who is still to come." *9* Whenever the living beings give glory and honor and thanks to the one sitting on the throne, the one who lives forever and ever, *10* the twenty-four elders fall down and worship the one who lives forever and ever. And they lay their crowns before the throne and say, *11* "You're worthy, O Lord your God, to receive glory and honor and power. For you created everything, and it is for your pleasure that they exist and were created."

Explained in a nutshell!

God loves you more than you could possibly know. That's why Jesus died for your sins. But not everyone accepts that salvation. For those people, there's a terrible time of punishment coming. But for Christians, Jesus has already paid for that punishment. He won't make you endure this terrible time, but will keep you safe from it. In a flash, John is taken up to Heaven! He is allowed to see what Heaven is like, and the scene is awesome! He can only describe the sight as one like flashing, colorful gemstones, and a circled rainbow! He sees humans with crowns as well as mysterious creatures which we don't see on earth. Most importantly, although He doesn't actually see God, God *is* there. Holy, constant worship of Him is the emphasis in Heaven.

Key verse: 4:1

Key word: Holy

Focus locus—themes and threads throughout!

- **Heaven**—Heaven is the home of God, Jesus, all the good angels, and all people who have died trusting their lives to God. Where Heaven is, no one knows. *Revelation* gives us many insights into Heaven. We know that Heaven isn't just sitting on a cloud somewhere—playing a harp when we die. No, Heaven is a place to be close to God. Since God is everything good and holy, Heaven must be a wonderful place. You'll still be you in Heaven—your talents, personality, and everything that makes you unique. You just won't ever die, age, or be sad.

Getting to know Jesus!

- *Lord God Almighty*—(see chapter 1)

- *He who was, is, and is to come*—(see chapter 1)

- *The Creator of all things*—(see chapter 1 and John 1:1-3)

Nuts to crack—terms to know!

- **Door**—(see John 14:6, and 'open door' in chapter 3)

- **Throne**—Where a king sits!

- **Jasper**—Clear and sparkling like a diamond!

- **Carnelian**—Red.

- **Rainbow**—Beautiful and with an emerald green hue! This rainbow surrounds God's throne—over it (maybe representing His mercy) and under it (maybe His grace)! There's no rainbow like this on the earth. A full rainbow can usually only be seen when you're high in the sky, as in flight! (See Gen. 9:13-17.)

- **Emerald**—Bright green!

- **Twenty-four Elders**—A Heavenly group of individuals. We can't be sure who they are, but God knows! They aren't angels. Whoever they are, they are rewarded and resting from their labors. (See I Chron. 24:3-5.)

- **White garments**—(see chapter 3)

- **Crowns**—(see chapter 2)

- **The seven lampstands**—(see chapter 1)

- **The Sevenfold Spirit of God**—(see chapter 1)

- **The sea of glass**—We can't be sure what some of these Heavenly things are, but apparently there's a smooth, diamond-like sea of something like glass before God's throne. Maybe it's a 'sea' of sparkling crystal. Whatever it is, it's beautiful. As seas separate nations on earth, this sea keeps everything and everyone at a distance from an awesome and holy God! This sea reflects His awesome holiness! (See chapter 15.)

- **The four Living beings**—Again, we're looking at Heavenly things through earthly eyes and we can't be sure what some of these things are. From their appearance, we know that these creatures aren't like anything on earth, yet are described as looking like a mixture of the four types of wild creatures on earth: creatures that fly (eagle), creatures that can be tamed and used for service (ox), things that are wild (lion), and humans. Whatever they are, these Heavenly creatures watch everything that comes before God. They see all things. They're concerned with earth, and unlike the elders, they're in constant motion and never rest! (Cp. Isa. 6:2; Ezek. 1:4-14; See Rev. 9:7-10!)

- **Holy**—Holy doesn't mean perfect. Neither does it mean you lead a perfect (or perfectly boring!) life and never commit any sins. Holy just means *separate*. What's that got to do with the word holy? God wants you to live as far apart from sin as you can by the power of His Holy Spirit. As a Christian, if you let the Spirit lead you, you'll better know what does—and doesn't—please God. Being holy then, means to learn to live pleasing to God. Study your Bible. Listen to the Holy Spirit within you, and you'll learn how to live holy—apart from sin. When you do sin, God is ready to forgive you, but living holy is your ultimate goal.

Backpack for the road—Principles to Ponder!

- *God never forgets His promises or His people!*—Some have said: 'God said it, I believe it, and that settles it!'. It could be better said: 'God said it—that settles it!'. If God makes a promise, He'll keep it. He has promised to get you to Heaven, to protect you from the devil, to supply your needs (but not all your wants!), as well as many other things He tells you in His Word. Learn God's promises and trust His faithfulness. He'll never leave you or forsake you! (See chapter 21.)

Journal for the journey—My reflections!

- ✓ How do I picture Heaven? Who are the 10 people I want to see first when I get there?

- ✓ How can I live holy for God without appearing *too* holy and turning off my friends?

- ✓ What particular sins do I need God's Spirit to help me with?

- ✓ What particular promises in the Bible mean the *most* to me?

- ✓ Would I *want* to know the future? Even the bad things?

- ✓ Why was the first thing John saw in heaven the throne?

- ✓ Why was *holy* the one and only word the Living beings kept repeating?

- ✓ What pleasure does God enjoy because He created me?

- ✓ How do I show my continual praise to my God?

Chapter 5

"Second Snapshot of Heaven!"
(The Lamb's book: what a worship service!)

1 And I saw a scroll in the right hand of the one who was sitting on the throne. There was writing on the inside and the outside of the scroll, and it was sealed with seven seals. *2* And I saw a strong angel, who shouted with a loud voice: "Who is worthy to break the seals on this scroll and unroll it?" *3* But no one in Heaven or on earth or under the earth was able to open the scroll and read it. *4* Then I wept because no one could be found who was worthy to open the scroll and read it. *5* But one of the twenty-four elders said to me, "Stop weeping! Look, the Lion of the tribe of Judah, the heir to David's throne, has conquered. He is worthy to open the scroll and break its seven seals." *6* I looked and I saw a Lamb that had been killed but was now standing between the throne and the four living beings and among the twenty-four elders. He had seven horns and seven eyes, which are the seven spirits of God that are sent out into every part of the earth. *7* He stepped forward and took the scroll from the right hand of the one sitting on the throne. *8* And as he took the scroll, the four living beings and the twenty-four elders fell down before the Lamb. Each one had a harp, and they held gold bowls filled with incense—the prayers of God's people! *9* And they sang a new song with these words: "You're worthy to take the scroll and break its seals and open it. For you were killed, and your blood has ransomed people for God from every tribe and language and people and nation. *10* And you have caused them to become God's Kingdom and his priests. And they will reign on the earth." *11* Then I looked again, and I heard the singing of thousands and millions of angels around the throne and the living beings and the elders. *12* And they sang in a mighty chorus: "The Lamb is worthy—the Lamb who was killed. He is worthy to receive power and riches and wisdom and strength and honor and glory and blessing." *13* And then I heard every creature in Heaven and on earth and under the earth and in the sea. They also sang: "Blessing and honor and glory and power belong to the one sitting on the throne and to the Lamb forever and ever." *14* And the four living beings said, "Amen!" And the twenty-four elders fell down and worshiped God and the Lamb.

Explained in a nutshell!

There are things in Heaven we'd never know about if *Revelation* didn't show them to us. God has a plan to deal with the many problems we see in the world today. That plan is called *redemption*. Redemption is a process that takes place over time. In Heaven, John sees a mysterious sealed book. No one was worthy to loose the seals and open the book until Jesus stepped forward. He is a sacrificed yet living Lamb who sees and knows all things, and deserving of *all* praise. Because He died and fulfilled God's plan for Heaven and earth, He alone could open the book and reveal the contents. All of Heaven rejoiced because God's plan could now move forward!

Key verse: 5:5

Key word: Worthy

Focus locus—themes and threads throughout!

- **Prayer**—Prayer isn't just talking to God, but letting God speak to you in your heart. God doesn't just want you to come to Him when you're in a jam. He wants you be in the spirit of prayer all day. If you'll just keep God online, He'll be right there when you need to instant-message Him! Prayer doesn't have to be on your knees either. Prayer is a heart thing! Pray for everything—that way when good things happen, you can praise God for answering. And when God says 'no' to some things, at least you can know it wasn't because you didn't ask!

- **The Redemption of the earth!**—This old earth doesn't belong to you or me. It doesn't belong to the nations either. We're just renting space for a while! Earth doesn't belong to the devil either, even though with all the bad things happening in the news we might think so. God owns the earth, and put mankind in charge of it when He created all things. But when Adam and Eve sinned in the Garden of Eden, they gave their 'in charge' over to the devil. That's one reason evil seems to be in charge of our world today. But someday Jesus is going to return and redeem (take back) Planet Earth and everything in nature will be as God intended at the beginning! (See chapters 6, 14 & 20 and Rom. 8:19-23.)

- **Worship**—Worship is giving God the praise and honor He deserves *as God*. It also includes our thanksgiving for saving us from our sins, and calling us His children. You not only worship God in church, you worship Him by doing what He wants to you do in your life. How do you know what He wants you to do? Study His word, hang with other Christians, and pray. Do these and you'll get a pretty good idea! All of God's creation worships God by simply doing what He put each thing here to do. Shouldn't you worship this way too? (See Rev. 4:8-11; 7:12-17; 11:15-18; 19:1-6.)

Getting to know Jesus!

- *The Lion of Judah*—Judah was one of the twelve families of Israel. From Judah's family Jesus came. Jesus is seen as the lion because He is King, He is powerful and royal, and He's awesome and kind of frightening. While we should never fear God (if we're His children) we should never forget that He is an awesome God! (See Gen. 49:8-12.)

- *The Root of David*—Jesus wasn't just from the family of Judah. He was from one specific family in Judah—the kingly family of David. Jesus isn't just one of the distant children of King David. As God who is outside of time, Jesus can be the root, or source of David's family line. As a human, Jesus was born a thousand years after King David. But as God, Jesus—the Creator of all things—existed as the root of David, long before David (or anyone else) ever existed. (See II Sam. 5; John 1:1-3.)

- *The Lamb killed*—While Jesus is described as a mighty and powerful lion, He is also called a lamb. The lamb was the animal of sacrifice. It was killed in place of a sinful person in the Old Testament. The little lamb was gentle and innocent, white and pure. This is the picture of the Jesus who died in your place for sin. (See John 1:29; Gen. 22:7; Ex. 12.) Here, the Lamb is *alive*, standing in *strength*, and with *ever-searching* eyes!

Nuts to crack—terms to know!

- **Throne**—Where a king sits.

- **The scroll**—This scroll is probably the title deed to the earth. It is long, and already written. When mankind lost the authority over the earth after sinning in the Garden of Eden, no one could claim that authority again—except the Lamb (Jesus) who died to pay for all our sins. Only Jesus—the Creator and rightful owner—could redeem Planet Earth! The unwinding of this scroll results in the terrible judgments of the Great Tribulation. These judgments are the 'labor pains' our world must endure before the birth of The Kingdom! (See John 1:1-3; Matt. 24; and Rev. 20.)

- **Seal**—This is one of the most important words in *Revelation*. When something is sealed, it is protected. When you seal a letter, you protect its journey. Roman law also required a will to be rolled up and sealed seven times. In times past, people sometimes sealed letters with a wax stamp to guard their letters. That stamp was a seal that included their name. The seal both guarded the letter and identified the one to whom that letter belonged. That seal was never to be removed until the letter reached its destination. What a beautiful picture this is of God sealing His children—guaranteeing their protection—until they reach their Heavenly destination! Never forget—as a Christian, God has sealed you with his 'mark' of ownership (see chapter 13). You belong to Him, and He'll get you safely home (Eph. 1:13; 4:30; Rom. 8:28-39).

- **Angels**—(see chapter 1)

- **Elders**—(see chapter 4)

- **Living beings**—(see chapter 4)

- **The seven horns**—Horns always represent *power*. Seven stands for *completeness*. The fact that the Lamb (Jesus) has seven horns means that He has complete power. Here, He'll use His power to redeem the earth from the sin that Adam and Eve brought into the world. (See Eph. 1:18-23.)

- **The seven eyes**—Eyes, of course, represent sight. The Lamb (Jesus) with seven eyes means that He has insight into everything that can be known. Jesus knows the right way to do everything. He isn't just all-powerful, He is all knowing.

- **The Sevenfold Spirit**—(see chapter 1)

- 'Amen'—(see chapter 3)

Backpack for the road—Principles to Ponder!

- *God will get you home*—As a Christian, God has sealed you. That means that He guarantees to get you safely to heaven when you die. (John 14:2-3) But this only applies to genuine Christians—make sure you're the real thing! (See chapter 7 and Rom. 8:31-39.)

Journal for the journey—My reflections!

- ✓ How can I pray better? Do I have a quiet time and place with God?

- ✓ Do I *really* listen when God speaks to my heart?

- ✓ Do I thank God even when He says *no* or *wait?*

- ✓ In what ways can I worship or praise God *better?*

- ✓ How is prayer like incense whose smoke rises up to God?

- ✓ How do I praise God? What talents do I offer Him?

- ✓ How does being *sealed* by God make me feel?

- ✓ Knowing that Jesus is *always* watching me, are there things I should, or should *not*, be doing? What are they?

Chapter 6

"The Great Tribulation!"
(Peeling the seals—the four horsemen of doom!)

_1_ As I watched, the Lamb broke the first of the seven seals on the scroll. Then one of the four living beings called out with a voice that sounded like thunder, "Come!" 2 I looked up and saw a white horse. Its rider carried a bow, and a crown was placed on his head. He rode out to win many battles and gain the victory. _3_ When the Lamb broke the second seal, I heard the second living being say, "Come!" _4_ And another horse appeared, a red one. Its rider was given a mighty sword and the authority to remove peace from the earth. And there was war and slaughter everywhere. _5_ When the Lamb broke the third seal, I heard the third living being say, "Come!" And I looked up and saw a black horse, and its rider was holding a pair of scales in his hand. _6_ And a voice from among the four living beings said, "A loaf of wheat bread or three loaves of barley for a day's pay. And don't waste the olive oil and wine." _7_ And when the Lamb broke the fourth seal, I heard the fourth living being say, "Come!" _8_ And I looked up and saw a horse whose color was pale green like a corpse. And Death was the name of its rider, who was followed around by the Grave. They were given authority over one-fourth of the earth, to kill with the sword and famine and disease and wild animals. _9_ And when the Lamb broke the fifth seal, I saw under the altar the souls of all who had been martyred for the word of God and for being faithful in their witness. _10_ They called loudly to the Lord and said, "O Sovereign Lord, holy and true, how long will it be before you judge the people who belong to this world for what they have done to us? When will you avenge your blood against these people?" _11_ Then a white robe was given to each of them. And they were told to rest a little longer until the full number of their brothers and sisters—their fellow servants of Jesus—had been martyred. _12_ I watched as the Lamb broke the sixth seal, and there was a great earthquake. The sun became as dark as black cloth, and the moon became as red as blood. _13_ Then the stars of the sky fell to the earth like green figs falling from trees shaken by mighty winds. _14_

And the sky was rolled up like a scroll and taken away. And all of the mountains and all of the islands disappeared. *15* Then the kings of the earth, the rulers, the generals, the wealthy people, the people with great power, and every slave and every free person—all hid themselves in the caves and among the rocks of the mountains. *16* And they cried to the mountains and the rocks, "Fall on us and hide us from the face of the one who sits on the throne and from the wrath of the Lamb. *17* For the great day of their wrath has come, and who will be able to survive?"

Explained in a nutshell!

Redemption of the earth won't come without suffering and death. John now sees the results on earth of the opening of the sealed book in Heaven. One by one Jesus removes the seals. The events of the Great Tribulation begin—the events that will lead to God redeeming the earth from the sin that Adam and Eve's sin plunged it into. The Great Tribulation promises peace, but brings war, famine, earthquakes, falling stars, and much death. But death for the children of God means they'll be in Heaven. God's love is never far from those who trust Him. God's anger is never far from sin. Interestingly, those in Heaven are curious about what's going on back on the earth, and God asks them to wait.

Key Verse: 6:17

Key Word: Given

Focus locus—themes and threads throughout!

- Antichrist—*Anti* means *against,* or *in place of.* Antichrist will be a human being who'll come to the world scene someday and appear to have the peaceful solution to all the world's problems. He'll appear as the wonderful 'answer-man' the world has been waiting for. But he'll fool nearly everyone. He'll be the devil's best work. Antichrist will be full of arrogant pride and selfishness! He'll lead the world into terrible—not peaceful—times. He'll be against everything Jesus stood for, and will call himself God! He'll be more frightening than Hitler, Sadaam Hussein, or any other dictator who ever lived. (See chapter 13, and Daniel 8:23-24; 11:36-45; John 5:43; II Thes. 2:3-12.)

- **Dying for your faith!**—Could *you*? (See 'martyr' in chapter 2.)

- **The Great Tribulation**—This is the time of great trouble that will someday come upon Planet Earth when Antichrist promises to lead the world into peace. The description of the awful time is pretty much what the rest of *Revelation* is all about. This 'tribulation' or trouble will last about seven years, and billions of people will die from war, disease, murder, and starvation. If you think problems like AIDS, Ebola, global warming, hurricanes like *Katrina*, Avian flu viruses, and terrorism are bad today, wait until the Great Tribulation! Many  Christians believe Jesus will call Christians to Heaven before this awful time (see 'Rapture' in chapter 3). Only the Second Coming of Jesus will end this suffering, and the career of the wicked Antichrist. (See Isa. 13; Dan. 9:24-27; Jer. 30:7; Isa. 13:6-13; 24:17-23; Matt. 24:5-29.)

- **The sovereignty of God!**—Sovereignty simply means that God has the right and the power to do anything and everything He wants. This would be frightening if God weren't also holy and good. So, when bad things happen, it's not because God can't control things. It's just because even though He can, He sometimes chooses to let bad things happen for good reasons He doesn't explain to us. Knowing that God is sovereign will mean a lot to those who go through the Great Tribulation! (See chapters 1 and 3.)

- **Prayer**—see chapter 5.

Getting to know Jesus!

- *The Lamb's wrath!*—We've seen that the Lamb is Jesus, and wrath is great anger. But how can a gentle lamb become angry? Jesus got angry when He was on earth. What made Him angry then makes Him angry now—sin. Sin is everything that is against God. God hates sin! Sin makes God angry. This anger isn't a temper tantrum, but the settled attitude of a holy God against that which is unholy. If you're a Christian, God sees your sins as *forgiven*. Because Jesus died for your sins, God will never be angry with you again.

- *Sovereign Lord*—This means that Jesus has absolute and total power over everything! He's in control—of life, death, the Great Tribulation—even Heaven and Hell! (See chapter 1.)

- *Holy & True*—(see chapters 1 & 3)

Nuts to crack—terms to know!

- **Seals**—(see chapter 5)

- **Living beings**—(see chapter 4)

- **The white horse**—The rider here isn't Jesus! The rider is Antichrist! The white horse stands for peace and purity (see chapter 19). The rider here has a bow, but no arrow—he comes promising peace without war! Most of the world will fall for this promise—it'll sound so good! But even though he promises peace, Antichrist is the devil's main man, and the devil is the father of lies! (See II Thes. 2:1-12.)

- **The red horse**—This horse stands for war and blood! Possibly 4 billion people will die during this awful time. The sword here is the *assassin's* (murderer's) sword! Terrorism in the world today is just a preview of a worse time to come! Antichrist's promise of peace will be a lie, and war will follow. The results of the wars in the Great Tribulation are what the rest of *Revelation* is about. (See Zech. 6:1-8.)

- **The black horse**—This horse stands for what results from most wars—famine. Food will run short during the Great Tribulation. Every year twenty million people starve to death, and half the world goes to bed hungry each night. But it will be worse in the Great Tribulation!

- **Pair of scales**—Scales represent balancing out something. Here, the scales are measuring out food because during the Great Tribulation food will be scarce, people will be starving, and the grocery store shelves will empty in a hurry!

- **A day's pay**—This would've been a Denarius—how much a person usually made working in one day when *Revelation* was written. Think about paying a whole day's wage for just a piece of bread! This measures to about 1200% inflation during this period, compared to 4% today!

- **Olive oil & wine**—This oil isn't what we put in our cars. Oil and wine refer to more than basic food. They refer to the luxuries that rich people in John's day could afford. The meaning here is that even though food will be scarce in the Great Tribulation, the rich people will still be able to afford the luxuries they're used to. Wealthy people will be affected less by the famines and wars—just as they are today. But eventually, the Great Tribulation will affect everyone on earth.

- **The pale green horse**—This horse stands for the final result of war and famine—death. Billions will die during this period from disease, war, famine, the beasts of the earth, and the murders committed by Antichrist. (See Ezek. 14:21; Matt. 24:3-8.)

- **The Grave**—Actually, this is called *Hades.* In Greek mythology, Hades was the brother of Zeus, and ruler of the underworld. Here, Hades stands for the unseen world of death. Billions will die during the Great Tribulation—many by starving!

- **One fourth**—This stands for God's mercy. How? Remember, God is in control. The Great Tribulation is mankind's sinfulness being punished, but God only allows destruction of one fourth—not all—of mankind. But things will get worse (see chapter 8).

- **White robes**—Many who turn to Christ during the Great Tribulation will be killed for their faith. In heaven, they cry for justice, and God patiently, lovingly tells them to *wait*—His plan must run its course. (Their prayers will be answered in the next chapter.)

- **Martyrs**—(see chapters 1, 2 and 3)

- **Black cloth or 'sackcloth'**—This, as well as an earthquake, happened when Jesus died for the sins of the world. It will happen again to a world that has *rejected* Him. Here, we also see asteroids falling from the sky. People are frightened into hiding, but not into salvation. This proves that no matter what God does to reach people, some will

continue to refuse Him. (See Matt. 24:7; 27:51; 28:2; Isa. 6:14; Joel 2:30-31. Cp. Rev. 9:20-21; 16:11.)

Backpack for the road—Principles to Ponder!

- *Redemption is costly. God gave His Son's life for you!*—God is holy. God also only does what is right. Because of this, God couldn't just save you from your sins by sneaking you past His decision that sin was so bad only death could defeat it. But not just any death. It must be the death of One greater than the power of the sins of every human being who ever sinned! So how did God save you, or redeem you from sin? He paid the death-cost Himself by sending His Son to die for your sins, my sins, and the sins of everyone who would trust their lives to Christ! Yes, becoming a Christian may have seemed free to you, but it cost God His Son! (See chapters 5 & 14 and John 3:16.)

- *God is sovereign, and in control of all things!*—(See chapters 1 & 9.)

- *Persecution from the world will increase the closer we get to Christ's return!*—Because the devil hates God, and God's children, he wants to stir up as much trouble for them as he can. The Bible tells us that no one knows when Jesus will return, but it tells us things to look for when His return is close. The devil can see these signs too, and when he realizes his time is short, he'll work even harder to stir up trouble. Because the devil can't hurt God, he chooses to hurt the next best thing—you and me—God's children. Everyone belongs to either God or the devil, so when non-Christians seem to be bringing more hurt, embarrassment, and insults to you, it just might be because Jesus is coming soon! (See chapters 2 & 3 and II Tim. 3:13.)

- *God always answers prayer; sometimes yes, sometimes no, often—wait!*—Just because you don't get everything you ask God for doesn't mean He doesn't hear you. He does hear you—every prayer you make. But God knows the future—you don't. Sometimes God sees that the answer you want from your prayer would bring harm or hurt to you. Sometimes He sees you're just not ready for what you want just yet. Because God knows exactly what's best for you—and when it's best for you—He either answers *yes, no,* or *wait.* But He always answers and expects you to trust Him to answer in the way that's best for you. (See Matt. 7:7, John 14:13-14 and chapter 5.)

- *Praying for justice is OK!*—Just as those in heaven are seen praying for justice toward their enemies, so you and I might sometimes wish God would punish the wicked. It's OK to feel this way. Just remember to let God do the punishing—it's not your job!

Journal for the journey—My reflections!

- ✓ Am I careful to watch out for false teachers of God's Word?

- ✓ Do I know my Bible well enough to recognize them?

- ✓ Am I being impatient for God to do something in my life? How might God respond to me about this?

- ✓ What things do I see in the world today that remind me of what's to come on earth someday?

- ✓ Why will the world so *easily* fall for Antichrist?

- ✓ Why does God punish *over time* and not all at once?

- ✓ Am I being persecuted for my faith? If not, why?

- ✓ Have I ever wanted to hide from God? Why?

- ✓ What answers to prayers am I *still* waiting for?

- ✓ Am I able to accept *no* as an answer, or do I continually try to get what I want?

- ✓ When I hear of AIDS, the Avian flu virus, diseases spread by rats, monkeys and other beasts, mass starvation, hurricanes like Katrina, terrorism and wars, do I remember that these are merely a *preview* of what's to come?

- ✓ Do I know people who refuse to become Christians no matter what things God sends into their lives? What can I do to help them?

Chapter 7

"Timeout—Part 1"
(So, will *anybody* survive this awful mess?)

1 Then I saw four angels standing at the four corners of the earth, holding back the four winds from blowing upon the earth. Not a leaf rustled in the trees, and the sea became as smooth as glass. *2* And I saw another angel coming from the east, carrying the seal of the living God. And he shouted out to those four angels who had been given power to injure land and sea, *3* "Wait! Don't hurt the land or the sea or the trees until we have placed the seal of God on the foreheads of his servants." *4* And I heard how many were marked with the seal of God. There were 144,000 who were sealed from all the tribes of Israel: *5* from Judah—12,000 from Reuben—12,000 from Gad—12, *6* from Asher—12,000 from Naphtali—12,000 from Manasseh—12, *7* from Simeon—12,000 from Levi—12,000 from Issachar—12, *8* from Zebulun—12,000 from Joseph—12,000 from Benjamin—12, *9* After this I saw a vast crowd, too great to count, from every nation and tribe and people and language, standing in front of the throne and before the Lamb. They were clothed in white and held palm branches in their hands. *10* And they were shouting with a mighty shout, "Salvation comes from your God on the throne and from the Lamb!" *11* And all the angels were standing around the throne and around the elders and the four living beings. And they fell face down before the throne and worshiped God. *12* They said, "Amen! Blessing and glory and wisdom and thanksgiving and honor and power and strength belong to your God forever and forever. Amen!" *13* Then one of the twenty-four elders asked me, "Who are these who are clothed in white? Where do they come from?" *14* And I said to him, "Sir, you're the one who knows." Then he said to me, "These are the ones coming out of the Great Tribulation. They washed their robes in the blood of the Lamb and made them white. *15* That is why they are standing in front of the throne of God, serving him day and night in his Temple. And he who sits on the throne will live among them and shelter them. *16* They will never again be hungry or thirsty, and they will be fully protected from the scorching noontime heat. *17* For the Lamb who stands in front of the throne will be their Shepherd. He'll lead them to the springs of life-giving water. And God will wipe away all their tears."

Explained in a nutshell!

While in the process of redeeming the earth from sin, God is still concerned for human beings who didn't escape the Great Tribulation at the Rapture. What will happen to them? Who will tell them of the salvation of Christ? Who will warn them of the Hell they face after death? It's the calm before the storm. The Great Tribulation is about to unfold—the time of terrible destruction and death upon the earth. But God will protect His own—even through this. 144,000 Jews are chosen to speak for God to a sinful world. God still cares for the people He created—even through this. These 144,000 will take the message of salvation through Jesus all over the world, and cause many to be saved. They will be murdered, but be greatly rewarded and comforted when they get to Heaven.

Key verse: 7:17

Key word: Sealed

Focus locus—themes and threads throughout!

- Salvation—Saved from what? What does it mean to be 'saved'? If you're saved, you're saved from sin—the thing that separates you from a holy God. As a Christian, you're already saved from sin's power to send you to Hell. Because God has given you His Holy Spirit, you have the power to be saved from sin's persistence (wanting to do things sometimes, which you know are wrong!). But that's a growing process! (Thank God for forgiveness!) Someday, when Jesus returns, you'll be saved from the presence of sin, and live in a nearly perfect world ruled by Jesus—the rightful King! (See chapters 14 & 19 and Acts 4:12.)

- Your protection in Christ!—Jesus didn't just save you from your past sins. He saved you from *all* your sins. This is the protection you have from ever worrying about going to Hell. Just remember what it cost God to save you, though—it cost Him the life of His Son Jesus. Never forget that cost when you think you can sin because it's no big deal. It is. (See Eph. 1:13-14, chapter 20, and *seal* in chapter 5.)

Getting to know Jesus!

- *The Lamb*—(see chapter 5)

- *The Shepherd*—We've seen Jesus as the Lamb. Here, He's the Shepherd. As a Shepherd, Jesus protects His flock (you, me, and all Christians) from the devil who would love to rip us to pieces! He's the Shepherd who loved his flock so much He was willing to die for them. What a loving Shepherd you and I have! (See John 10:11; Psalms 23.)

- *The Living God*—Jesus is the Creator of all life. Jesus is also God. God can't die, but Jesus *did* die. Don't try to understand this—just accept it because God said it's true. Because of this, when Jesus died for your sins, He was able to defeat death through His resurrection. Jesus is the Living God because He always existed, and will never die again. We can't understand this but it's still true.

Nuts to crack—terms to know!

- Angels—(see chapter 1)

- Four winds—Because wind stands for action, and the earth has four cardinal directions, these have to do with events that happen on the earth.

- Seals—A seal is a protection or guarantee of deliverance. These Jewish preachers will cover the world with the fiery message of salvation. As a result of their message, there will be an uncountable number of people who will become Christians during the Great Tribulation. Unfortunately, they will have to endure hell on earth in the process. (See Matt. 24:14; Dan. 3:1-26; Ezek. 9:3-4; Eph. 1:13; 4:30.)

- The 144,000—This mysterious group of people is going to appear on earth in the future Great Tribulation. Maybe they're even alive today! Although it will be a terrible time of great evil and death, God will still have some people who will stand up for Him and tell the world about Jesus. This group will number 144,000, and will be Jewish (see Gen. 49). They will be honest to the death and holy to the bone! God will permit them to be killed, but we'll see them in heaven in a later chapter! How they will know precisely which tribe of Israel they're from, we don't know.

But the order of the tribal names is interesting. The name meanings—read in order—roughly reveal the following message: "Praisers of God, looking upon the Son—a great number of them—blessed and happy. They wrestle against forgetfulness by hearing and obeying God—holding firm to their reward—looking toward another home, a greater one. They are sons of God's right hand—born at the end of the age." (See Deut. 33.)

- **Thrones**—where a king sits.

- **Palm branches**—Jews sometimes waved these before a king or royal figure. The palm branches were symbols of a great 'sweeping of the path' to make way for a king.

- **Elders**—(see chapter 4)

- **Living beings**—(see chapter 4)

- **Amen**—(see chapter 3)

- **Clothed in white**—Those in heaven are 'dressed' in the white purity of salvation—salvation only made possible by Mary's little Lamb. His blood made them—and makes *you*—holy and pure. (see chapter 3)

- **Great Tribulation**—(see chapter 6)

Backpack for the road—Principles to Ponder!

- *If you're truly a Christian, God will never let you go!*—(See chapter 5.)

- *God allows bad things to happen to good people—always for a reason!*— God knows the future. You and I don't. God is also fully in control of all things—including what the devil does! So, when God permits bad things to happen to good people, He has a reason. That reason is always good, though it may not seem like it to the person bad things happen to. God may someday explain His reasons for letting bad things happen to good people, but He doesn't always do it today. Just trust Him. He's in control. (See chapters 10, 11, 13 & 22 and Rom. 8:28.)

Journal for the journey—My reflections!

- ✓ The 144,000 were willing to die in telling strangers about Christ. For whom would *I* be willing to die?

- ✓ *The calm before the storm.* What does this expression mean?

✓ How do I measure up to the description of the 144,000?

✓ What color is my Christian 'clothing' that the world sees?

✓ How do I answer my friends who say there are *many* ways to be saved and get to Heaven?

✓ Since all my sins are forgiven, can I live any way I want? Why? Why not?

✓ Will there really be tears in heaven?

✓ How has something that seemed bad in my life turned out for *good?* Did I learn to trust God more *because* of that?

✓ How might I answer friends who think they will wait to be saved *during* the Great Tribulation? (See II Thes. 2:10-12; Heb. 2:3; 7:25.)

Chapter 8

"Trumpets of Doom!"
(Or, 'I thought angels only brought *good news?*')

1 When the Lamb broke the seventh seal, there was silence throughout Heaven for about half an hour. *2* And I saw the seven angels who stand before God, and they were given seven trumpets. *3* Then another angel with a gold incense burner came and stood at the altar. And a great quantity of incense was given to him to mix with the prayers of God's people, to be offered on the gold altar before the throne. *4* The smoke of the incense, mixed with the prayers of the saints, ascended up to God from the altar where the angel had poured them out. *5* Then the angel filled the incense burner with fire from the altar and threw it down upon the earth; and thunder crashed, lightning flashed, and there was a terrible earthquake. *6* Then the seven angels with the seven trumpets prepared to blow their mighty blasts. *7* The first angel blew his trumpet, and hail and fire mixed with blood were thrown down upon the earth, and one-third of the earth was set on fire. One-third of the trees were burned, and all the grass was burned. *8* Then the second angel blew his trumpet, and a great mountain of fire was thrown into the sea. And one-third of the water in the sea became blood. *9* And one-third of all things living in the sea died. And one-third of all the ships on the sea were destroyed. *10* Then the third angel blew his trumpet, and a great flaming star fell out of the sky, burning like a torch. It fell upon one-third of the rivers and on the springs of water. *11* The name of the star was Bitterness. It made one-third of the water bitter, and many people died because the water was so bitter. *12* Then the fourth angel blew his trumpet, and one-third of the sun was struck, and one-third of the moon, and one-third of the stars, and they became dark. And one-third of the day was dark and one-third of the night also. *13* Then I looked up. And I heard a single eagle crying loudly as it flew through the air, "Terror, terror, terror to all who belong to this world because of what will happen when the last three angels blow their trumpets."

Explained in a nutshell!

God is patient. He puts up with sin much longer
than you or I would. But God won't wait forever
to punish evil. When His mercy and grace finally run out, the horrors of judgment are beyond
what we might really want to know. Jesus carefully removes the 7th seal from the book. Again,
there is an awesome calm in Heaven before the
destruction on earth. Seven mighty angels
appear before God with trumpets of doom! The
first four angels blow their trumpets. Suddenly,
an earthquake rocks the earth, and fiery bloody
hail destroys one third of God's living earthly
creation. Waters are poisoned, and the sun,
moon, and stars begin to dim, but the worst is
yet to come.

Key verse: 8:5

Key word: Silence

Focus locus—themes and threads throughout!

- **Sin has an effect on the earth itself**—sin not only brought suffering and
  death to mankind, it also brought decay and death to all God's creation.
  Like people, plants and animals die too. But they didn't sin—man did.
  (See chapter 20 and Romans 8:19-23.)

Nuts to crack—terms to know!

- **The Lamb**—(See chapter 5)

- **Incense burner**—An instrument for holding burning coals of fire.

- **Altar**—The altar was where the sacrificed animal was killed before God.
  It was the holiest place in the temple. It was at the altar that blood and
  forgiveness of sin were linked.

- **Incense**—A sweet fragrance offered up to God. (See Lev. 16:12-13.) At
  this altar is kept all the prayers from God's children. God hasn't forgotten
  any of their prayers, or *yours*. Remember that! (See 5:8.)

- **Saints**—A saint isn't just a holy dead person that people decide to honor and make a statue of! A saint is any Christian. If you've trusted your life to Christ, you're bound for Heaven and you're a saint! The word actually means *holy*, or *set apart from sin to God*, and is a pretty good description of how saints should act!

- **Bitterness**—The word here is actually wormwood—a very bitter and poisonous plant. The waters of earth will be made bitter and poisonous! Jesus predicted these frightening sights in the sky! (See Luke 21:25-26.)

- **One third**—Not all, but part. Here, God is showing two things. First, He shows you His mercy. Part—not all—is affected. Second, He shows you His justice. He'll act against sin. He'll not be patient forever. Earlier, God destroyed only one fourth of the earth. Now, His judgment becomes more intense. (See chapter 6; compare the judgments on Egypt in Ex. 7, 9, 10, 15.)

- **The single eagle**—Either a great bird or an angel (See chapter 12.)

- **Terror**—Things are going to get much worse as the Great Tribulation continues.

Backpack for the road—Principles to Ponder!

- *There is a limit to God's patience, and it's pretty scary when it comes!*—As mentioned, God is patient with you and me, but He won't wait forever without punishing a sinful world.

- *When God does punish sin, He's not being unfair or unkind*—Sin is a violation of God's holiness, and the deserved punishment is death. Instead of blaming God for death and suffering in the world, we might thank Him that He spares us from more than we deserve! (See chapter 16.)

Journal for the journey—My reflections!

- ✓ Do I have a 'pet sin' that God hasn't disciplined me for yet? Why is He waiting to deal with it? Why am *I*?

- ✓ Is God being mean when He punishes sin? What about parents and teachers? Why? Why not?

- ✓ Why does God sometimes wait so long to answer my prayers? Does He always answer? How do I know?

Chapter 9

"Grasshoppers from Hell!"
(You've *never* seen anything like these before!)

1 Then the fifth angel blew his trumpet, and I saw a star that had fallen to earth from the sky, and he was given the key to the shaft of the bottomless pit. *2* When he opened it, smoke poured out as though from a huge furnace, and the sunlight and air were darkened by the smoke. *3* Then locusts came from the smoke and descended on the earth, and they were given power to sting like scorpions. *4* They were told not to hurt the grass or plants or trees but to attack all the people who did not have the seal of God on their foreheads. *5* They were told not to kill them but to torture them for five months with agony like the pain of scorpion stings. *6* In those days people will seek death but won't find it. They will long to die, but death will flee away! *7* The locusts looked like horses armed for battle. They had gold crowns on their heads, and they had human faces. *8* Their hair was long like the hair of a woman, and their teeth were like the teeth of a lion. *9* They wore armor made of iron, and their wings roared like an army of chariots rushing into battle. *10* They had tails that stung like scorpions, with power to torture people. This power was given to them for five months. *11* Their king is the angel from the bottomless pit; his name in Hebrew is Abaddon, and in Greek, Apollyon—the Destroyer. *12* The first terror is past, but look, two more terrors are coming! *13* Then the sixth angel blew his trumpet, and I heard a voice speaking from the four horns of the gold altar that stands in the presence of God. *14* And the voice spoke to the sixth angel who held the trumpet: "Release the four angels who are bound at the great Euphrates River." *15* And the four angels who had been prepared for this hour and day and month and year were turned loose to kill one-third of all the people on earth. *16* They led an army of 200 million mounted troops—I heard an announcement of how many there were. *17* And in my vision, I saw the horses and the riders sitting on them. The riders wore armor that was fiery red and sky blue and yellow. The horses' heads were like the

heads of lions, and fire and smoke and burning sulfur billowed from their mouths.
_18_ One-third of all the people on earth were killed by these three plagues—by the
fire and the smoke and burning sulfur that came from the mouths of the horses. _19_
Their power was in their mouths, but also in their tails. For their tails had heads like
snakes, with the power to injure people. _20_ But the people who did not die in these
plagues still refused to turn from their evil deeds. They continued to worship
demons and idols made of gold, silver, bronze, stone, and wood—idols that neither
see nor hear nor walk! _21_ And they did not repent of their murders or their witchcraft or their immorality or their thefts.

Explained in a nutshell!

The Bible gives us very little detail about Hell. We probably wouldn't really
want to know everything. But now, God is giving us a preview, and it isn't
pretty. The fifth angel sounds his trumpet, and the devil himself is thrown
down out of access to Heaven to the fiery Hell that is the underworld. From
there, grasshopper creatures—like we've never seen before—are led by a
demon king and attack people who refuse to worship the true God. People
suffer such pain that they wish to die, but for five months they are _unable_ to
die! The sixth trumpet angel lets loose the largest and strangest army ever
seen, to cross the Euphrates River. Another one-third of the people die, leaving earth's population reduced by more than half! But even at this frightening period of the Great Tribulation, people refuse to repent of their sins.

Key verse: 9:21

Key word: One-third

Focus locus—themes and threads throughout!

- Hell—(See 'The Second Death'—chapters 2 & 20.) Hell wasn't created
  for people. Hell was created for the devil and his angels who sinned
  against God long ago. But people who choose not to follow Christ will
  end up in Hell. Picture Hell as a place where everything that's good,
  happy, and beautiful is missing. It's a place of evil, darkness, sadness,
  pain, and it's forever. Worst of all, it's a place where God and all your
  Christian friends will never be! (See Luke 16:19-31; Matt. 5:22-30; 10:28;
  13:41-42.)

- Demons!—Demons are probably angels which chose to follow Satan
  (the devil) in sinning against their Creator (God) in the long ago. Many

demons roam earth and do the devil's work of bringing misery to people. These demons, like the good angels, will never age, die, or reproduce. When God finally sends them all to Hell, they will be there forever and forever.

Nuts to crack—terms to know!

- **Star**—The star here is none other than Satan—the devil himself—being thrown down out of the Heavens (see Luke 10:18; Isa. 14:12). For more detail on this throwing down of Satan, see Rev. 12:7-9.

- **Key**—Authority (See chapter 1.)

- **Bottomless pit**—Hell or Hades. This may be one section of Hell where *unusually* horrible creatures are kept. (See Luke 8:26-31; Jude 6.)

- **Locusts**—You might think of locusts as a type of grasshopper, but these are creatures from Hell turned loose on the earth! The have descriptions that go far beyond locusts we know, and they bring pain and suffering to earth! These locusts are crowned with Hell's crowns. They move with great speed, and from them there's no escape. They are extremely fierce, can't be hurt, and are frightening to look at.

- **Scorpions**—Earthly scorpions sting with their tail, and the sting is very painful! The pain brought by the strange locusts will be much worse!

- **Five months**—God limits the suffering, but allows it nonetheless. For five months people in the Great Tribulation will suffer without being able to die! Why does God permit this? To give man an idea of what Hell is like—suffering without death! This preview is limited—Hell is forever!

- **A seal**—(see chapter 5)

- **Crowns**—(see chapter 2)

- **Abaddon/Apollyon**—These names in two languages mean 'to destroy'!

- **Euphrates**—This is the famous river in modern Iraq. History started here with the culture of Mesopotamia. It looks as if history might end here, too! Evidently there are some very wicked angels in charge of Iraq who are just waiting to unleash the powers of Hell!

- **Burning sulfur**—The word is brimstone. Brimstone is like a piece of fiery hot charcoal! Imagine the heat and pain if you were to try and hold this in your hand! (See chapter 14.)

- **Repentance**—(see chapters 2 & 16)

- **Sexual immorality**—The word is fornication. It means sex outside of marriage. (See chapter 14.)

- **Witchcraft**—We have superstitions and black magic today. Much of it involves the devil. It will be much worse in the future. Witchcraft here can also include the illegal use of drugs, such as marijuana, cocaine, heroin, etc. Any substance that causes you to lose control of knowing and doing what is *right* can cause you to do evil. Don't get involved with such things.  Though your friends may see them as fun pastimes, or popular, they are not Christian in any way! (See Deut. 18:10-14.)

Backpack for the road—Principles to Ponder!

- *God is sovereign over all things—even history is 'His-story'!*—(See chapters 1 and 6.) Remember—even when things in your life seem out of control, God is still in charge. History is His story. (See also Eph. 1:9-11; Isa. 46:9-11; Prov. 19:21; Job 42:2.)

- *When your heart gets hard, it's nearly impossible to turn to Christ*—God gave you a conscience. Your conscience is what tells you right and wrong. If you keep going against your conscience, you'll finally stop hearing it. Your heart will get hard. When you're no longer concerned with right and wrong, it's hard for Christ to speak to your heart. To keep turning down Christ's invitation to be saved is frightening. The time may eventually come when you won't hear Him at all, and the chance for salvation will be gone forever. Listen to your conscience and God's call when you're young! (See chapter 16 and Prov. 6:15; 29:1, and II Thes. 2:10.)

Journal for the journey—My reflections!

✓ Do I have friends who think there's no Hell? How might I describe it to them?

✓ Why is Hollywood so caught up in the subject of *demons* and *evil?*

✓ How are Hell's locusts different from locusts on earth?

✓ Am I watching references to the Euphrates Rivers area (Iraq) in the news?

✓ Are there sins I should repent of?

✓ Why does God warn me against getting involved in *harmful drugs, witchcraft, demons,* and *evil spirits?*

✓ Do I have friends who continue to turn down Christ's offer of salvation?

✓ Do I know people who've stopped hearing their consciences because they've committed a particular sin so long they no longer feel it's wrong? Will it be more difficult to help such people see their errors?

✓ How does God show His concern for Planet Earth in this chapter?

✓ Why don't people seem to call on God for salvation during the Great Tribulation?

Chapter 10

"Halftime!"
(And they're asking you to eat a *book*?)

1 Then I saw another mighty angel coming down from Heaven, surrounded by a cloud, with a rainbow over his head. His face shone like the sun, and his feet were like pillars of fire. *2* And in his hand was a small scroll, which he had unrolled. He stood with his right foot on the sea and his left foot on the land. *3* And he gave a great shout, like the roar of a lion. And when he shouted, the seven thunders answered. *4* When the seven thunders spoke, I was about to write. But a voice from Heaven called to me: "Keep secret what the seven thunders said. Do not write it down." *5* Then the mighty angel standing on the sea and on the land lifted his right hand to Heaven. *6* And he swore an oath in the name of the one who lives forever and ever, who created Heaven and everything in it, the earth and everything in it, and the sea and everything in it. He said, "God will wait no longer. *7* But when the seventh angel blows his trumpet, God's mysterious plan will be fulfilled. It will happen just as he announced it to his servants the prophets." *8* Then the voice from Heaven called to me again: "Go and take the unrolled scroll from the angel who is standing on the sea and on the land." *9* So I approached him and asked him to give me the little scroll. "Yes, take it and eat it," he said. "At first it will taste like honey, but when you swallow it, it will make your stomach sour!" *10* So I took the little scroll from the hands of the angel, and I ate it! It was sweet in my mouth, but it made my stomach sour. *11* Then he said to me, "You must prophesy again about many peoples, nations, languages, and kings."

Explained in a nutshell!

Sports events have halftimes, and so does *Revelation*. As bad as things seem to be on the earth at this point, *Revelation* takes a timeout to remind us that God is still in charge of everything—both in Heaven and on earth. But the worst is yet to come. Another mighty angel now holds the book that has been unsealed. It's smaller since much of *Revelation* is completed. Seven booming thunders speak some message to John, which God chose not to tell us. The  mighty angel stands upon the earth and sea and announces that God's patience with a sinful world is at an end. The 7th trumpet angel will finish the judgment on the earth. John learns that although the awful judgment is near its end (good news) the end of it will be the worst of all (bad news). He must keep writing!

Key verse: 10:7

Key word: Mystery

Focus locus—themes and threads throughout!

- Redemption—(see chapter 5)

- Prophecy—Prophecy means to speak about the future.

Getting to know Jesus!

- *The One who lives forever*—Jesus is eternal! (See chapter 1.)

Nuts to crack—terms to know!

- Rainbow—The rainbow around this good angel's head is a reminder of the rainbow of promise given to Noah. God promised to never again destroy the world with a flood. As the Great Tribulation gets more severe, God reminds us that the earth *will* survive, and that He has not forgotten His promise. (See Gen. 9:13-15, and Rev. 4:2-3.)

- The small scroll—This book may be the same book you saw in chapter 5—the title deed to the earth and what must happen to redeem our world from evil. If so, it's now smaller since some of the things that must happen will already have happened by this chapter. Maybe this book is *Revelation* itself, and the events of the Great Tribulation, which is now nearly half over.

- **The Seven Thunders!**—We know absolutely nothing about these! Do you know what? No one else does either!

- **Sealing**—(see chapter 5)

- **Swearing an oath**—You aren't supposed to swear. But this swearing isn't saying inappropriate words. Here, the angel makes an oath—a very strong promise—to guarantee something is going to happen. The angel is taking back possession of Planet Earth from the power of Satan! (See Deut. 11:24; Matt 5:34-37; Heb. 6:13-18.)

- **God's mysterious plan**—(see chapter 1)

- **Prophets/prophesy**—(see chapter 1 & 18)

Backpack for the road—Principles to Ponder!

- *God doesn't always explain everything to us, and only He knows why!*— Did you ever ask God 'why' about something? Though God always does what's right, some things that happen to us may not seem right. When we ask God 'why' things happen (like death, pain, and disappointments) He doesn't usually explain. Someday He will. When you get to Heaven, you can ask Him all the 'why's' you want. When He explains them to you, what seemed unfair on earth will seem perfectly right in the end. Trust God. He's always right. (See chapters 7, 11, 13 & 19 and I Cor. 7:32; Mark 13:32-33; Dan.12:8-9.)

- *Even though God is sovereign, we're still responsible to do what we can!*—It's hard to understand some things about God. For example, if He's in control of everything, does that make you and me puppets to do His will? No. While God is sovereign, and doesn't really need our help, a part of His grand plan is that you and I do everything we can to bring His plan into action. For example, if God knows how long you'll live, do you still need to eat? Of course you do! Your actions are part of His plan too. This is hard to figure, but if you just do your best (to be a good Christian) and trust God for the rest—this is enough to know. (See chapters 11 & 17 and Phil. 2:12. See Rev. 13:10!)

- *God is even sovereign over death itself!*—(see chapters 1, 6 & 9.)

Journal for the journey—My reflections!

- ✓ What are some things happening in my life right now that I'm having to trust God for?

- ✓ Do I love God so much that I even thank Him for the food, water, and the air He has given me to survive, or do I take these for granted?

- ✓ If God is in control of things, is mankind still responsible for terrorist attacks, abortions, murders, and other types of evil?

- ✓ When was the last time I did something for God that I really *didn't* look forward to doing?

- ✓ What are some things that look '*sweet*' to me now which could end up being very '*bitter*'?

- ✓ Why does God choose *not* to tell us some things, and to answer '*no*' to some of our prayers?

Chapter 11

"God's Dynamic Duo!"
(Two guys who really *will* 'stand up' for God!)

1 Then I was given a measuring stick, and I was told, "Go and measure the Temple of God and the altar, and count the number of worshipers. *2* But do not measure the outer courtyard, for it has been turned over to the nations. They will trample the holy city for 42 months. *3* And I will give power to my two witnesses, and they will be clothed in sackcloth and will prophesy during those 1,260 days." *4* These two prophets are the two olive trees and the two lampstands that stand before the Lord of all the earth. *5* If anyone tries to harm them, fire flashes from the mouths of the prophets and consumes their enemies. This is how anyone who tries to harm them must die. *6* They have power to shut the skies so that no rain will fall for as long as they prophesy. And they have the power to turn the rivers and oceans into blood, and to send every kind of plague upon the earth as often as they wish. *7* When they complete their testimony, the beast that comes up out of the bottomless pit will declare war against them. He'll conquer them and kill them. *8* And their bodies will lie in the main street of Jerusalem, the city which is called "Sodom" and "Egypt," the city where their Lord was crucified. *9* And for three and a half days, all peoples, tribes, languages, and nations will come to stare at their bodies. No one will be allowed to bury them. *10* All the people who belong to this world will give presents to each other to celebrate the death of the two prophets who had tormented them. *11* But after three and a half days, the spirit of life from God entered them, and they stood up! And terror struck all who were staring at them. *12* Then a loud voice shouted from Heaven, "Come up here!" And they rose to Heaven in a cloud as their enemies watched. *13* And in the same hour there was a terrible earthquake that destroyed a tenth of the city. Seven thousand people died in that earthquake. And everyone who did not die was terrified and gave glory to the God of Heaven. *14* The second terror is past, but look, now the third terror is coming quickly. *15* Then the seventh angel blew his trumpet, and there were loud voices shouting in

Heaven: "The whole world has now become the Kingdom of your Lord and of his Christ, and he'll reign forever and ever." *16* And the twenty-four elders sitting on their thrones before God fell on their faces and worshiped him. *17* And they said, "We give thanks to you, Lord God Almighty, the one who is and who always was, for now you have assumed your great power and have begun to reign. *18* The nations were angry with you, but now the time of your wrath has come. It is time to judge the dead and reward your servants. You'll reward your prophets and your holy people, all who fear your name, from the least to the greatest. And you'll destroy all who have caused destruction on the earth." *19* Then, in Heaven, the Temple of God was opened and the Ark of his covenant could be seen inside the Temple. Lightning flashed, thunder crashed and roared; there was a great hailstorm, and the world was shaken by a mighty earthquake.

Explained in a nutshell!

God has shown us that He'll have 144,000 men spreading the word of Christ during the Great Tribulation. Now He shows us two very special men who can do mighty miracles. The earthly city of Jerusalem now becomes the focus as God tells John to measure its temple and people. John finds out that for the last half of the Great Tribulation, evil people who hate God will violate the temple there. God will raise up two spokesmen to preach His message—even now. These two men will be supernaturally protected, and will do great miracles like what Moses and Aaron did in Egypt. Only when God allows it will these men be murdered. Their bodies will lie unburied in Jerusalem's streets for three and one half days. In the middle of a great celebration, suddenly, they'll stand up and go up to Heaven! A great earthquake kills 7000 people in Jerusalem, and the people in Heaven begin to see the end of the Great Tribulation. As the 7th angel blows his trumpet, Heavenly voices begin to praise God as earthquakes and hail rock the earth!

Key verse: 11:15

Key word: Great

Focus locus—themes and threads throughout!

- **Resurrection!**—The word 'resurrection' means *to stand up again.* Someday, the bodies of every person who ever lived will stand up again. Every person will spend forever in a new body that can't be destroyed.

Some people will spend forever in Heaven. Others—in Hell. (See chapter 1, and John 5:25-29; Dan. 12:2; Isa. 41:4.)

- **The Kingdom**—(see chapters 1, 5, 6, 14 & 20)

- **God's judgment**—(See chapter 3.) God is holy. God hates sin and evil. God is patient, and doesn't always judge sin and evil right away, but make no mistake—He'll judge it! The longer He waits, the more terrible the judgment! (See Nah. 1:2-8; II Thes. 1:6-10.)

Getting to know Jesus!

- **'The One who is, and was...'**—(See chapter 1.) Never forget, Jesus is outside of time. He was before time and will exist after time ends.

Nuts to crack—terms to know!

- **Reeds**—Picture these as measuring sticks, like our rulers or yardsticks. Here, John measures for *judgment.*

- **The Holy/great city**—Jerusalem!

- **The two witnesses**—God will have His 'super preachers' even in this time of judgment known as 'The GreatTribulation'. Why there are only two, or who these two are, we can't be sure. Some think they might be Old Testament heroes such as Moses or Elijah which God brings back to the future. We just don't know who they'll be. (Cp. Moses & Elijah—I Kings 17, and II Kings 1.) The whole world will probably see them on *CNN* when they die, but God will bring them back to life in less than a week! These two individuals will have power over *nature, death* and *disease*! They are great preachers who will only be killed when *God* decides. Like Jesus—they will rise from the dead! Also, as with Jesus, when they do rise, there will be a great earthquake! (See Zech 4:4-14; Mal. 3:1-3; Deut. 34:5-6; Matt. 17:3; 28:2.)

- **42 months/1260 days**—This equals 3.5 years, or one-half of the tribulation period. (See chapters 12 and 13.)

- **Prophesy**—Speak for God.

- **Sackcloth**—Did you ever see burlap? It looks like old grain bags—very coarse and scratchy. You wouldn't want to wear clothes made from it! Long ago, people wore sackcloth to feel uncomfortable about their sinfulness when they prayed. It was a symbol of humility, sorrow for sin, and repentance. It helped them get rid of too much pride when they spoke to a holy God. (See Isa. 22:12; Matt. 11:21.)

- **Olive trees**—These trees represent Israel, or the Jewish people. Olive trees grow well in Israel. (See Zech. 4:2-14.)

- **Lampstands**—(see chapter 1)

- **Plagues**—Diseases.

- **Beast**—(see chapters 6 and 13)

- **Bottomless pit**—(see chapter 17)

- **Sodom & Egypt**—Jerusalem. Here, the holy city is being described as like two very wicked places. God says that Jerusalem is no longer holy, but during the Great Tribulation will become as wicked as any other place.

- **They rose to Heaven in a cloud**—The word is ascension—to ascend means to rise up. Jesus ascended to Heaven when He left Earth after His resurrection.

- **Remnant**—(see chapter 12)

- **Elders**—(see chapter 4)

- **Wrath**—great anger!

- **Reward**—(see 'crowns' in chapter 2)

- **The Ark of the Covenant**—If you saw the movie *Indiana Jones & the Raiders of the Lost Ark*, you know that the ark was a gold box with angels on top. God had the Hebrews make it to represent His holiness and His mercy. God doesn't enjoy punishing people, but God is holy, and He hates sin! (See Ex. 16, 25 & 30.)

Backpack for the road—Principles to Ponder!

- *We are responsible for how we live each day, though God has numbered them!*—If you believe that God knows everything, does He also know what you'll do today? Yes, He does. He also knows how many days you'll live. That number is certain. But He still expects you to eat and take care of yourself. Even though God knows everything you'll do today, you're still responsible to do what you're able to please Him. (See chapters 10, 17, and Ps. 90:12.)

- *Do what God's Word says—if for no other reason than God said to!*—You don't need to *understand* God in order to *obey* God. When God instructs you—through your conscience, or through the Bible—you'll want to trust and obey. God is always right—even if you don't understand all His ways. (See Prov. 3:5.)

- *When 'bad' seems to win, remember that evil isn't the 'rest of the story'!*—Your life is like one of those movies where you wonder if the hero is ever going to survive. But usually, the hero wins in the end. Don't get discouraged when friends hurt you, or when you just can't seem to get a break. God has seen how your story ends—He wins. So do you! (See chapters 7, 10, 13 & 22 and Ps. 23.)

- *When God doesn't shake your tree, it should make you worry—not feel good!*—Have you ever heard the expression: *only the tree bearing fruit gets shaken*? Did you ever see anyone shaking a fruitless tree? Not likely. God is like a parent who cares enough about His children that He disciplines them when they need it. Though you might think you'd enjoy parents who left you alone, you'd probably feel they didn't care about you. You should be glad when God allows tough times in your life. This is evidence He does care. More often, it's the devil's kids God leaves alone. (See chapter 3 and Luke 4:29; John 6:37; III John 10.)

- *When evil doesn't leave you alone, it might be a sign you're living right!*—This is much like what you just read. Someone has said that it's light that makes the rats run away, because darkness is what they love. When evil people react against you, it might be because you're good! Never forget that! (See Matt. 12:27-30.)

Journal for the journey—My reflections!

- ✓ What are some things my conscience bothers me about?

- ✓ How can I be *sure* I'm following Christ's instructions?

- ✓ Why does God let bad things happen to good people?

- ✓ How do I feel when someone who loves me corrects me?

- ✓ How do I feel when they say *nothing* and let me do anything I want?

- ✓ When bad people treat me poorly, do I consider this a compliment to my witness?

- ✓ If God gave me power over nature, life, and death, could I be trusted with it? How do I know?

Chapter 12

"Previewing the Cast for the Blast!"
(So, do dragons *really* eat children?)

1 Then I witnessed in Heaven an event of great significance. I saw a woman clothed with the sun, with the moon beneath her feet, and a crown of twelve stars on her head. *2* She was pregnant, and she cried out in the pain of labor as she awaited her delivery. *3* Suddenly, I witnessed in Heaven another significant event. I saw a large red dragon with seven heads and ten horns, with seven crowns on his heads. *4* His tail dragged down one-third of the stars, which he threw to the earth. He stood before the woman as she was about to give birth to her child, ready to devour the baby as soon as it was born. *5* She gave birth to a boy who was to rule all nations with an iron rod. And the child was snatched away from the dragon and was caught up to God and to his throne. *6* And the woman fled into the wilderness, where God had prepared a place to give her care for 1,260 days. *7* Then there was war in Heaven. Michael and the angels under his command fought the dragon and his angels. *8* And the dragon lost the battle and was forced out of Heaven. *9* This great dragon—the ancient serpent called the Devil, or Satan, the one deceiving the whole world—was thrown down to the earth with all his angels. *10* Then I heard a loud voice shouting across the Heavens, "It has happened at last—the salvation and power and kingdom of your God, and the authority of his Christ! For the Accuser has been thrown down to earth—the one who accused your brothers and sisters before your God day and night. *11* And they have defeated him because of the blood of the Lamb and because of their testimony. And they were not afraid to die. *12* Rejoice, O Heavens! And you who live in the Heavens, rejoice! But terror will come on the earth and the sea. For the Devil has come down to you in great anger, and he knows that he has little time." *13* And when the dragon realized that he had been thrown down to the earth, he pursued the woman who had given birth to the child. *14* But she was given two wings like those of a great eagle. This allowed her to fly to a place prepared for her in the wilderness, where she would be cared for and protected from the dragon for a time, times, and half a time. *15* Then the dragon tried to drown the woman with a flood of water that flowed from its mouth. *16* But the earth helped her by opening its mouth and swallowing the river that gushed out from the mouth of the dragon. *17* Then the dragon became angry at the woman, and he declared war against the rest of her children—all who keep God's commandments and confess that they belong to Jesus. *18* Then he stood waiting on the shore of the sea.

Explained in a nutshell!

Evil, death, and suffering will get worse and worse as time goes on. Now that John has seen what's in store for Jerusalem, the city, he must see what's in store for Israel the country. John sees Satan—as a bloodthirsty dragon—continually trying to destroy Israel. But Israel gives birth to Jesus, whom Satan can't defeat. Israel is protected from the old devil for the last 3.5 years of the Great Tribulation. Finally, Michael—Heaven's greatest angel—fights and throws Satan down to the earth. Knowing his time is short, Satan does his best to hurt mankind—especially Israel. He now raises up his finest work—Antichrist!

Key verse: 12:10

Key word: Thrown down

Focus locus—themes and threads throughout!

- **Signs**—Signs tell you where you're going, and give you an idea of when you're getting close. God gives signs of His Second Coming so that you might know it's getting close, and look forward to the day by living in a way that's pleasing to Christ. When you see the signs of increased evil in the world, famine, disease, and the focus on Israel—don't be afraid—be excited. Jesus is coming! (See Matt. 16:2-3.)

- Israel—This means that little country in the Middle East. Israel is the country that has always been close to God's heart. In ancient days they were called the Hebrews. Today, the people in Israel are called the Jews. The Jews have had many hard times in their history. The Holocaust was just one of these. *Revelation* tells us that the hardest time Israel will ever have will be during the Great Tribulation. Watch the news concerning Israel. That nation is God's clock telling us how close we are to the Second Coming of Jesus. (See Romans 9.)

- **How the devil tricks us!**—The devil doesn't trick you into sin with things that look bad. You wouldn't bite! No, he tricks us with things that look *good*. You must study your Bible and listen to your conscience to know when good isn't what it appears! Remember—the devil appears as an angel of light—not darkness! But the devil is already a defeated enemy. Treat him like one! (Matt. 25:41; Isa. 24:21; John 16:11; II Cor. 10:4-5; 11:14-16; Eph. 6:11; I Pet. 5:8; Luke 10:18.)

Getting to know Jesus!

- *The Male-child*—Jesus was born a human boy. While He was completely God in His spirit, He was also completely human in His physical appearance. He grew up, too. It's hard to picture Jesus as a child, but He once was.

- *Ruler of all nations with a rod of iron*—(see chapter 2).

- *The Lamb's blood*—As the Lamb of God (see chapter 5), only the blood of Jesus could forgive sins. The blood of the lamb used for sacrifice in the Old Testament was only temporary until Jesus could come and die. Only the blood of God's Lamb can satisfy God's holy requirements. (See Heb. 9:12-14; 10:4; Rev. 7:4.)

Nuts to crack—terms to know!

- **The woman surrounded by the sun, moon & stars**—This is Israel. *Stars* here represent the twelve families of Israel. We know this from the Book of Genesis. (See Gen. 37:4-11; Isa. 66:7-8; Romans 9-11.)

- **Seven heads & ten horns**—(see chapter 13)

- **Crowns**—(see chapter 2)

- Stars—These are different from the first stars. These refer to all the evil angels who followed Satan. These may be what we now call demons.

- **The Wilderness**—Somewhere God will hide His people (Israel) to protect them from the devil and Antichrist. We don't know where this will be, but it may be in the country of Jordan, east of Israel. God has always protected His people in times of great trouble. (Cp. Matt. 24:16-20; I Kings 17:1-6.)

- **1,260 days ('a time, times, and half a time')**—This is 3.5 years—(42 months) exactly one-half of the seven-year Great Tribulation. Even though this will be the most terrible time in history, it *is* limited. God is always in control. This terrible time *will* have an end! (See chapters 11 & 13.)

- Michael—One of God's special angels! He's called an 'archangel', an angel of the highest rank! God has billions of angels to serve Him, but the Bible names only a few, and they're very high in the rank of angels! Michael is near the top! (So was Satan before he sinned against God and was thrown out of Heaven.) Michael seems to have a special job of protecting Israel. (See Daniel 10:13; 12:1; Jude 9.)

- **The one who accused your brothers & sisters**—Clearly, the old devil still has access to the gates of Heaven. There, he tries to keep reminding God of every sinful act we might commit. God ignores him. Not because we're good, but because we're forgiven by the blood of the Lamb! (See Job 1.) By the way, you have now reached the middle verse in *Revelation*!

- **The 'great eagle'**—This may be a real eagle, or maybe it stands for an airplane or something else that flies. Whatever it is, it will be *large*, and *protective* of God's people. (See Exodus 19:4; Deut. 32:11-12.)

- **Remnant**—Remnant here means *survivor.* A remnant is a leftover. A remnant of cloth or a remnant of an old house is what's left at the end. God's remnant here is the leftover Jewish people (the 144,000?) at the end of history. The rest of *Revelation* is how God cares for them during the terrible Great Tribulation.

- **Dragon/Devil/Serpent/Accuser**—Names for Satan. Why is he called a dragon? Maybe because of his fierceness, or because dragons are usually linked to destruction and war. Why is he called an 'accuser'? Because the devil seems to enjoy bringing up every bad thing you do and telling it to God (Job 1:6-12). Just because you are forgiven all your sins doesn't mean the old  devil won't still try to accuse you of every one of them all over again! (See Isa. 14; John 8:44; 12:3; Ezek. 28; Gen. 2:4-25, and chapter 2.)

- **Terror**—Things are going to get much worse as the Great Tribulation goes on.

- **Flood**—A flood of water can happen very quickly. *Speed*—not water— is the key here.

Backpack for the road—Principles to Ponder!

- *Things in the world will get worse the closer we get to Christ's return!*— The devil may be evil, but he's not stupid! Satan can see the signs of the end of history, too. He knows his time as troublemaker on Planet Earth is nearing an end. Because he knows this, he wants to work even harder creating evil. When you watch the news and see more and more things that are so bad you can't believe they're happening, just remember—this is a sign that Jesus is coming soon, and the devil knows it! (See II Tim. 3:13, and chapters 1 and 19.)

- *As we get closer to Christ's return, watch the world's focus on Israel!*— Sometimes the Jews are called God's *chosen people.* God loves all His children, but He has always loved the nation Israel in a special way. Israel is the focus of the whole Old Testament. Because of this, the devil hates Israel *most.* Keep watching the news about Israel. The closer to the Second Coming of Jesus, the more both God and the devil will focus their attention on Israel! (See Zech. 12:2.)

Journal for the journey—My reflections!

- ✓ Does it seem that things in the world have gotten worse? How?

- ✓ Am I noticing more mention of Israel in the news? Does the world's hatred of Israel seem to be increasing?

- ✓ How can I remain true to my faith in a world getting more sinful?

- ✓ *It's OK—everybody's doing it! Just once can't hurt.* How do these expressions reflect the way the world tries to deceive?

- ✓ How can I tell that things are *wrong* when they sometimes appear *good* to me?

- ✓ What would the devil be accusing me of in Heaven before God right now?

- ✓ Why is God ignoring him?

- ✓ Am I seeing more and more evil in the world today? What is this telling me?

- ✓ Why did so many angels choose to follow Satan?

- ✓ Why does the devil hates Jesus so much?

- ✓ Am I afraid to die? Why? Why not?

Chapter 13

"The Devil's Greatest Hits!" (And their tattoos from hell!)

_1_ And now in my vision I saw a beast rising up out of the sea. It had seven heads and ten horns, with ten crowns on its horns. And written on each head were names that blasphemed God. _2_ This beast looked like a leopard, but it had bear's feet and a lion's mouth! And the dragon gave him his own power and throne and great authority. _3_ I saw that one of the heads of the beast seemed wounded beyond recovery—but the fatal wound was healed! All the world marveled at this miracle and followed the beast in awe. _4_ They worshiped the dragon for giving the beast such power, and they worshiped the beast. "Is there anyone as great as the beast?" they exclaimed. "Who is able to fight against him?" _5_ Then the beast was allowed to speak great blasphemies against God. And he was given authority to do what he wanted for forty-two months. _6_ And he spoke terrible words of blasphemy against God, slandering his name and all who live in Heaven, who are his temple. _7_ And the beast was allowed to wage war against God's holy people and to overcome them. And he was given authority to rule over every tribe and people and language and nation. _8_ And all the people who belong to this world worshiped the beast. They are the ones whose names were not written in the Book of Life, which belongs to the Lamb who was killed before the world was made. _9_ Anyone who is willing to hear should listen and understand. _10_ The people who are destined for prison will be arrested and taken away. Those who are destined for death will be killed. But do not be dismayed, for here is your opportunity to have endurance and faith. _11_ Then I saw another beast come up out of the earth. He had two horns like those of a lamb, and he spoke with the voice of a dragon. _12_ He exercised all the authority of the first beast. And he required all the earth and those who belong to this world to worship the first beast, whose death-wound had been healed. _13_ He did astounding miracles, such as making fire flash down to earth from Heaven while everyone was watching. _14_ And with all the miracles he was allowed to perform on behalf of the first beast, he deceived all the people who belong to this world. He ordered the people of the world to make a great statue of the first beast, who was fatally wounded and then came back to life. *15* He was permitted to give life to this statue so that it could speak. Then the statue commanded that anyone refusing to worship it must die. *16* He required everyone—great and small, rich and poor, slave and free—to be given a mark on the right hand or on the forehead. *17* And no one could buy or sell anything without that mark, which was either the name of the beast or the number representing his name. *18* Wisdom is needed to understand this. Let the one who has understanding solve the number of the beast, for it is the number of a man. His number is 666.

Explained in a nutshell!

Good and evil have always fought against each other. We've seen that as the end of the age nears, God raises up some very special people to fight evil and represent Israel. But the devil will raise up his special ones, too. They'll have power to do miracles. John sees all of the great world empires—energized by Satan—which have tried to hurt Israel. The final enemy is the devil's masterpiece—Antichrist. Antichrist apparently tries to copy Jesus by pulling off a fake resurrection. It fools the world. Everyone except God's children worships Antichrist as a god for the last half of the Great Tribulation. God lets them fall for this trick. Helping Antichrist will be another man known as the False Prophet. Both men are called beasts. The False Prophet can also do miracles and fool the world. He even builds a great statue to Antichrist and makes it seem alive! The number of Antichrist's name will equal 666.

Key verse: 13:8

Key word: Blaspheme

Focus locus—themes and threads throughout!

- **Antichrist!**—(see chapter 6)

- **God's sovereignty!**—(see chapters 1, 6 and 9)

- **Signs**—(see chapter 12)

Getting to know Jesus!

- **The Lamb killed**—We saw in chapter 5 why Jesus is called a Lamb. The lamb was the main animal of sacrifice in the Old Testament. It was killed in place of people when God's showed His punishment for sin. Here, we see the Lamb who had been killed alive and well! Jesus died once for our sins, but He lives forevermore as our Savior! (See chapters 1 & 12.)

Nuts to crack—terms to know!

- **Sea**—This doesn't mean the literal sea here. Here, the sea stands for the restless nations of the earth. (See chapter 17, and Matt. 13:47.)

- **The two beasts!**—These two men are called 'beasts' because they are fierce and cruel. One beast is Antichrist (see chapter 6). The other beast is Antichrist's partner called 'the False Prophet'. He's a prophet because he speaks messages about the present and future. But he's called false because he speaks for the devil (so does Antichrist)—not for God. His messages are lies (the devil is called 'the father of lies!'), but the wicked people living at this time will believe his words. The world will think these two men are leading them out of this time of great trouble into a time of great peace. But in reality, these two men will lead the world into the devil's lap. Into Hell. (See chapter 6, and Matt. 24:24; II Thes. 2:3-11; II Cor. 11:13-15.)

- **The seven heads**—These heads represent the seven great enemy nations that have tried to hurt Israel down through history. Satan energizes them all. (See chapter 17, Dan.2:25; Dan.7 & 8.)

- **The ten horns**—Horns represent power (see chapter 5). These are the ten presidents, rulers, governments, or maybe ten sections of the world at the end of history. Some people think they'll be ten particular countries in Europe. (See Dan. 2:44.)

- **Crowns**—In Chapter 2 we saw crowns represent Heavenly rewards. Here, crowns represent earthly honor and authority. These crowns represent the power given to the ten horns (whatever they are) at the end of history. Clearly, all these crowns are on one head—the last world empire of history. (See Dan. 2:44.)

- **Blaspheme**—This word means to do or say something that is especially insulting toward God! All sin and evil is bad, but like wicked actions people do in the world—some are particularly awful! Antichrist, powered by Satan, will be an expert at especially wicked insults and actions against God!

- **The leopard**—The leopard is a symbol of speed, agility, and cunning. This describes how quickly and convincingly Antichrist will fool mankind and take over the world. As the leopard's color is white, brown, and black, so Antichrist may represent all three colors of the human race in his rulership. (See Dan. 2.)

- **The bear**—The bear is a symbol of crushing power. This describes the strength Antichrist will have as far as authority to rule given to him by the world. He'll crush any who oppose him! (See Dan 2.)

- **The lion**—The lion symbolizes royalty, majesty, and fierceness. This describes the kingship which the world will hand over to Antichrist. Promising peace, he'll bring destruction! He'll fool the world! (See Dan 2.)

- **The fatal wound was healed**—Could this be the devil's attempt to copy the resurrection of Jesus? (See II Thes. 2:8-12.)

- **Dragon**—(see chapters 2 & 12)

- **Forty-two months**—This is 3.5 years (see chapters 11 & 12).

- **The Book of Life**—(see chapters 3 & 20)

- **Great statue**—An image is something that stands for something else. When you see your reflection in a mirror, you see your image. The False Prophet will reflect the personality and desires of Antichrist. They'll be twin partners in crime and evil. The False Prophet's job will be to build up the Antichrist's image! (See Matt. 24:15-21; Dan. 2.)

- **The 'mark'**—Antichrist's mark or a tattoo is a permanent way to tell the world a message by advertising it on your body. Since it's usually permanent, and something you wear everywhere you go, it's a message you want the world to never forget when it sees you. It identifies you with that message. At the end of history, Antichrist will require everyone to get a permanent identification mark on his or her head and hand so that the rest of mankind will know that person belongs to him! This mark will be a permanent badge of dedication and loyalty to Antichrist (and Satan!), and the ticket to Hell for every person who gets it! (See Deut.6:8. Compare God's mark in Rev 14:1.)

- **Number of the beast!**—We are told the number (666), but how that relates to the name of Antichrist, we don't know. It'll probably be his name in Latin or Greek. People living at the end of history will understand. (See chapters 2, 3 & 19, and Dan. 12:4,10.)

Backpack for the road—Principles to Ponder!

- *God is always in control*—Sometimes He allows bad for a good reason! (See chapter 6, 7, 10, 11 and 22 .)

- *Be careful about miracles*—The devil can do them, too! (See chapters 2, 3, 12, 16 and 17; Acts 13:6-12; Matt. 7:15-23; 24:4-5; II Pet. 2:1-3, 10-21; II Cor.11:13-15; II Thes. 2:9-12.)

Journal for the journey—My reflections!

- ✓ Why does the world enjoy cursing and blaspheming God's name?

- ✓ Does it bother me to hear others take God's name in vain? How do I respond to them when they do it in front of me?

- ✓ Why is Satan so determined to destroy mankind and the earth?

- ✓ Are many of the world rulers today influenced by the devil?

- ✓ Why might God not want me to get tattoos, body piercings, or to cut carvings in my skin?

- ✓ What do I see happening in the world today that might lead to the *mark* of Antichrist, where everyone must have their own ID number?

- ✓ Why are people so quick to believe miracles and healings today?

- ✓ If God is in total control, why do I need to eat, study, or care about what happens at all?

Chapter 14

"Timeout—Part 2"
(Preview of the world's last great events!)

_1_ Then I saw the Lamb standing on Mount Zion, and with him were 144,000 who had his name and his Father's name written on their foreheads. _2_ And I heard a sound from Heaven like the roaring of a great waterfall or the rolling of mighty thunder. It was like the sound of many harpists playing together. _3_ This great choir sang a wonderful new song in front of the throne of God and before the four living beings and the twenty-four elders. And no one could learn this song except those 144,000 who had been redeemed from the earth. _4_ For they are spiritually undefiled, pure as virgins, following the Lamb wherever he goes. They have been purchased from among the people on the earth as a special offering to God and to the Lamb. _5_ No falsehood can be charged against them; they are blameless. _6_ And I saw another angel flying through the Heavens, carrying the everlasting Good News to preach to the people who belong to this world—to every nation, tribe, language, and people. _7_ "Fear God," he shouted. "Give glory to him. For the time has come when he'll sit as judge. Worship him who made Heaven and earth, the sea, and all the springs of water." _8_ Then another angel followed him through the skies, shouting, "Babylon is fallen—that great city is fallen—because she seduced the nations of the world and made them drink the wine of her passionate immorality." _9_ Then a third angel followed them, shouting, "Anyone who worships the beast and his statue or who accepts his mark on the forehead or the hand _10_ must drink the wine of God's wrath. It is poured out undiluted into God's cup of wrath. And they will be tormented with fire and burning sulfur in the presence of the holy angels and the Lamb. _11_ The smoke of their torment rises forever and ever, and they will have no relief day or night, for they have worshiped the beast and his statue and have accepted the mark of his name. _12_ Let this encourage God's holy people to endure persecution patiently and remain firm to the end, obeying his commands and trusting in Jesus." _13_ And I heard a voice from Heaven saying, "Write this down:

Blessed are those who die in the Lord from now on. Yes, says the Spirit, they are blessed indeed, for they will rest from all their toils and trials; for their good deeds follow them!" _14_ Then I saw the Son of Man sitting on a white cloud. He had a gold crown on his head and a sharp sickle in his hand. _15_ Then an angel came from the Temple and called out in a loud voice to the one sitting on the cloud, "Use the sickle, for the time has come for you to harvest; the crop is ripe on the earth." _16_ So the one sitting on the cloud swung his sickle over the earth, and the whole earth was harvested. _17_ After that, another angel came from the Temple in Heaven, and he also had a sharp sickle. _18_ Then another angel, who has power to destroy the world with fire, shouted to the angel with the sickle, "Use your sickle now to gather the clusters of grapes from the vines of the earth, for they are fully ripe for judgment." _19_ So the angel swung his sickle on the earth and loaded the grapes into the great winepress of God's wrath. _20_ And the grapes were trodden in the winepress outside the city, and blood flowed from the winepress in a stream about 180 miles long and as high as a horse's bridle.

Explained in a nutshell!

No matter how bad things seem to get, God is always in control. God is never surprised or defeated. Though He allows death, God will take care of every single person who trusts Him to be saved. Antichrist and the False Prophet of the Great Tribulation will bring great destruction upon the earth. What happens to the Christians who are killed during those awful 7 years? John now sees the 144,000 from chapter 7 in Heaven. There's great celebration at their arrival. God sees their death as a beautiful sacrifice. The end of history nears. God sends out another angel to spread the news to the whole world of His offer of salvation through Jesus. A second angel announces that the evil cities of earth are now doomed. A third angel warns that anyone worshipping Antichrist is also doomed—to an everlasting Hell. From this point on God tells mankind that it will be better to die than suffer the destruction ahead. For now, Jesus Himself will punish the earth in judgment, and the blood will be almost immeasurable!

Key verse: 14:19

Key word: Sickle

Focus locus—themes and threads throughout!

- Hell is forever!—(See chapters 2, 9, 17, 19 & 20.)

- **Grace**—Grace is getting something wonderful that you don't deserve. Grace was when God saved you from sin and Hell because His Son died on a cross, and you didn't have to. Grace acts out of mercy, and acts through love. (See chapter 1.)

- **Redemption**—(see chapter 5)

- **Crowns**—(see chapter 2)

- **The purpose of death**—We looked at death in chapters 1 and 2. But did you ever think that death could be *good*? When Adam and Eve sinned in the Garden of Eden, God sentenced them to death. Death not only puts an end to life, but for the person who dies, death puts an end to sin. Sin causes sickness, pain, old age, and feebleness. Would you prefer to get older and older and never be able to die? In this way, death is sometimes a blessing!

Getting to know Jesus!

- *The Lamb*—(see chapter 5)

- *The Son of Man*—(see chapter 1)

Nuts to crack—terms to know

- **Mt. Zion**—Mt. Zion is a large hill in Jerusalem. This probably stands for Heaven, though.—(see chapter 17)

- **The 144,000**—Every single one of them made it to Heaven. Not because of their actions, but because they were sealed by God. Like the 144,000, you cannot die until God is finished with you. (See chapter 7.)

- **Father's names written on their foreheads**—This was the *seal* of chapter 7. (See *names* in chapters 2, 3 & 19.)

- **Four Living beings & twenty-four elders**—(see chapter 4)

- **Redeemed**—Redeem means *to buy back*, or take back something. There is a cost involved. Jesus could not redeem you or me or Planet Earth without paying the demands of sin. Sin is everything opposed to our God of life. Sin results in death. That's why our bodies will eventually die if Jesus doesn't return soon. Jesus paid sin's demand (death) by dying for us and for our sins. So, He 'bought back' or redeemed what was lost in the Garden of Eden. (See chapter 5, 6 & 20 and I Cor. 6:20; Gal. 3:13; Luke 21:28.)

- **Spiritually undefiled & pure as virgins**—These 144,000 men will worship God alone, and apparently be virgins. God uses and honors and sexual purity. God made sex, and like everything else He made, it's good. God told us, though, that He allows sex only in a marriage between one woman and one man. God expects everybody who isn't married to be a virgin, or to live in sexual purity. He has a special job for these people. He has a special job for you too. (See chapters 2, 3 and 18; II Cor. 11:2-3; James 4:4.)

- **Special offering to God**—These are called God's first fruits.—The first fruits are the first part of the early harvest of grain. They were always dedicated to God to show He should receive the first and best of everything that He could be honored with.

- **The everlasting Good news**—The word gospel means *good news*. The gospel is that Jesus Christ died in the place of sinful mankind to satisfy the holy justice of an awesome God. This gospel is everlasting because it can never be replaced or improved on. Salvation in the Great Tribulation will be through the same method it is today—faith and trust in Jesus!

- **Babylon**—Babylon was the greatest city of ancient Mesopotamia. The city was awesome, full of wickedness, and very rich. Here, it stands for the world system at the end of history—wicked and wealthy. It may also refer to a specific major city in the Great Tribulation, but whatever it stands for, Babylon stands for sinfulness. (See Isa. 21:9; Jer. 50:35-38.)

- **Passionate immorality**—The word here is fornication. Fornication means sexual sinfulness. God doesn't look lightly on sexual sins. He expects you to remain pure outside of marriage. (See chapter 9.)

- **Statue**—(see chapter 13)

- **Mark**—(see chapter 13)

- **Wrath of God**—Great anger! (See Rom. 1:18.)

- **Fire & burning sulphur!**—Picture fiery, smoking, burning chunks of black rock (like coal) pounding down from Heaven on the earth.

- **Sharp sickle**—This is an instrument used in cutting grain. Here, it is used to 'harvest' the earth. God separates the righteous out from among the wicked. (See Matt. 13:37-43.)

- **Great winepress of God**—A winepress was where grapes were stomped to create juice used to make wine. The picture here is blood *pouring out*. It isn't a pretty sight.

- **The 'city'**—Jerusalem.

- **180 miles**—Interestingly, the country of Israel is about 180-200 miles long. Maybe this is the reference here. Whatever it is, this is an unbelievably frightening amount of blood!

Backpack for the road—Principles to Ponder!

- *Your actions prove your Christianity—they don't make you one!*—Dogs bark because they're dogs—they're not dogs because they bark. Many people can act Christian without actually being one. A Christian is someone who has given his or her life completely over to Christ. Because they have, they'll begin to act like a Christian because Christ lives in their heart. Their actions prove their Christianity, but don't make them a Christian any more than living in a garage makes you a car! (See chapter 7 and I Cor. 11:19; Dan. 12:10.)

- *Your works will follow you to Heaven where someday you'll be rewarded!*—You'll influence many people as a Christian. Some of them will influence others. This influence will go on long after you've died. Because of this, you'll still be earning rewards from your actions even after death. In this way, they'll follow you to Heaven where God will richly reward you someday! (See chapter 2; Luke 23:43; I Cor.15: 35-57; I Thes. 4:13-17.)

- *God overrules even death, and sometimes death is His blessing!*—(see chapters 1 and 13)

- *Hell is forever.* Notice that Hell is said to be a place of "no relief day or night", while those in Heaven "will rest from all their toils and trials." (See chapters 2 & 9.)

Journal for the journey—My reflections!

✓ Hell and Heaven are forever. Would I want to live forever and never die in the earthly body I have *now?* Why? Why not?

✓ Grace has been described as **God's Riches At Christ's Expense**. What does this mean to me?

✓ When was the last time I gave someone something good that they *didn't* deserve, and expected *nothing* in return?

✓ How can death ever be a *good* thing?

✓ Why was *Son of Man* Jesus' favorite title?

✓ Why is my sexual purity so special to God?

✓ Have I noticed that sexual purity is made fun of by most of my friends? How does this make me feel?

✓ What things in my life do I offer to God? My body? My time? My thoughts?

✓ What good deeds have I done that will follow *me* to heaven?

✓ Do I follow the Lamb's instructions in all I do and say? Where do I find these instructions? When was the last time I read them?

✓ Would I be willing to die rather than be forced to do something I knew was very wrong?

✓ Would people know I was a Christian by watching what I did and said for just one day?

✓ What can I learn from the 'blessings' in this book? (See: 14:13; 16:15; 20:6; 22:14)

Chapter 15

"The View from Heaven"
(Even when punishment seems *wrong*,
everything God does is *right*!)

1 Then I saw in Heaven another significant event, and it was great and marvelous. Seven angels were holding the seven last plagues, which would bring God's wrath to completion. *2* I saw before me what seemed to be a crystal sea mixed with fire. And on it stood all the people who had been victorious over the beast and his statue and the number representing his name. They were all holding harps that God had given them. *3* And they were singing the song of Moses, the servant of God, and the song of the Lamb: "Great and marvelous are your actions, Lord God Almighty. Just and true are your ways, O King of the nations. *4* Who won't fear, O Lord, and glorify your name? For you alone are holy. All nations will come and worship before you, for your righteous deeds have been revealed." *5* Then I looked and saw that the Temple in Heaven, God's Tabernacle, was thrown wide open! *6* The seven angels who were holding the bowls of the seven plagues came from the Temple, clothed in spotless white linen with gold belts across their chests. *7* And one of the four living beings handed each of the seven angels a gold bowl filled with the terrible wrath of God, who lives forever and forever. *8* The Temple was filled with smoke from God's glory and power. No one could enter the Temple until the seven angels had completed pouring out the seven plagues.

Explained in a nutshell!

Even though much of the earth and the environment will be destroyed during the Great Tribulation, God is right in everything He does. God alone is Creator. Sometimes He permits evil to get worse and worse so He can destroy it all at once. Seven last angels appear holding the seven last judgments of the

Great Tribulation. The Heavenly sea of glass is now ablaze as God's holy anger against a sinful world nears an end. All the Christians who were killed watch from Heaven as the end of history comes to earth. Even through such destruction, they know God is righteous and they praise Him—looking forward to His kingdom on earth. It's a holy moment in Heaven. The end of the world as we know it has arrived.

Key verse: 15:1

Key word: Last

Focus locus—themes and threads throughout!

- God's judgment—(see chapters 2, 3 & 11)

- The Great Tribulation—(see chapter 6)

Getting to know Jesus!

- *The Lord God Almighty!*—(see chapter 1)

- *King of the nations*—(see chapter 17) The Lord God is King of all kings.

Nuts to crack—terms to know!

- The sea of glass. Now the crystal sea is mixed with *fire*. God prepares His final execution for a sinful world. (See Ex. 24:10; Ezek. 1:22; Rev. 4:6.)

- Plagues—Diseases.

- Wrath—Great anger!

- Beast—(see chapter 13)

- Statue—(see chapter 13)

- Number representing his name—(see chapter 13)

- The song of Moses—(see Deut. 32)

- Living beings—(see chapter 4)

Backpack for the road—Principles to Ponder!

- *God's judgment is always fair*—even if seems not to be sometimes. As Creator, God has *absolute authority* over life and death. This final phase of judgment is a serious and holy moment in heaven. The seven last angels hold shallow bowls filled with judgment. The judgments will be *severe*, *swift*, and *more intense* than anything that has come before. They will answer the prayers of those we saw in Rev. 6:9-10. (See chapters 3 & 18; Psalms 37; Deut. 32:4.)

Journal for the journey—My reflections!

- ✓ Am I able to praise and thank God even when I feel as though He has been a little unfair to me?

- ✓ How do you think the watchers in heaven felt as God punished the earth and its people? How do you think *Jesus* felt?

- ✓ Have I ever thanked God for something He did in my life that I didn't understand?

- ✓ If I could write one song of praise to God, what things might it include?

Chapter 16

"Frogs Calling Men to War!"
(*Armageddon*—not the movie!)

1 Then I heard a mighty voice shouting from the Temple to the seven angels, "Now go your ways and empty out the seven bowls of God's wrath on the earth." *2* So the first angel left the Temple and poured out his bowl over the earth, and horrible, malignant sores broke out on everyone who had the mark of the beast and who worshiped his statue. *3* Then the second angel poured out his bowl on the sea, and it became like the blood of a corpse. And everything in the sea died. *4* Then the third angel poured out his bowl on the rivers and springs, and they became blood. *5* And I heard the angel who had authority over all water saying, "You're just in sending this judgment, O Holy One, who is and who always was. *6* For your holy people and your prophets have been killed, and their blood was poured out on the earth. So you have given their murderers blood to drink. It is their just reward." *7* And I heard a voice from the altar saying, "Yes, Lord God Almighty, your punishments are true and just." *8* Then the fourth angel poured out his bowl on the sun, causing it to scorch everyone with its fire. *9* Everyone was burned by this blast of heat, and they cursed the name of God, who sent all of these plagues. They did not repent and give him glory. *10* Then the fifth angel poured out his bowl on the throne of the beast, and his kingdom was plunged into darkness. And his subjects ground their teeth in anguish, *11* and they cursed the God of Heaven for their pains and sores. But they refused to repent of all their evil deeds. *12* Then the sixth angel poured out his bowl on the great Euphrates River, and it dried up so that the kings from the east could march their armies westward without hindrance. *13* And I saw three evil spirits that looked like frogs leap from the mouth of the dragon, the beast, and the false prophet. *14* These miracle-working demons caused all the rulers of the world to gather for battle against the Lord on that great judgment day of God Almighty. *15* "Take note: I will come as unexpectedly as a thief! Blessed are all who are watching for me, who keep their robes ready so they won't need to walk naked and ashamed." _16_ And they gathered all the rulers and their armies to a place called Armageddon in Hebrew. _17_ Then the seventh angel poured out his bowl into the air. And a mighty shout came from the throne of the Temple in Heaven, saying, "It is finished!" _18_ Then the thunder crashed and rolled, and lightning flashed. And there was an earthquake greater than ever before in human history. _19_ The great city of Babylon split into three pieces, and cities around the world fell into heaps of rubble. And so God remembered all of Babylon's sins, and he made her drink the cup that was filled with the wine of his fierce wrath. _20_ And every island disappeared, and all the mountains were leveled. _21_ There was a terrible hailstorm, and hailstones weighing seventy-five pounds fell from the sky onto the people below. They cursed God because of the hailstorm, which was a very terrible plague.

Explained in a nutshell!

As we've seen, there is a limit to God's patience. But there's also a limit to His anger. At last, God sends forth angels with the seven last judgments. The destruction upon the earth is rapid and terrible. Painful skin sores and scorching sunburn come upon the sinful people who worshipped Antichrist, but they refuse to repent of their sinfulness, and only curse God. The seas and rivers are turned into rotting blood, killing all the fish. Much of the world is plunged into darkness as giant hail pounds the earth, and there's a massive earthquake. A tremendous army marches west across the Euphrates River into Europe. The Beast and the False Prophet—by the power of 3 demon frog-spirits—gather together the remaining armies of earth—not to fight this army—but to challenge God Himself! But God is about to finish His judgments, as the wicked cities of the world hear their doom!

Key verse: 16:17

Key word: Great

Focus locus—themes and threads throughout!

- Repentance—To repent means to be so sorry for something that you look for a remedy and try to never do that something again. Repentance is what you do when you realize you can't meet God's requirement for holiness and you accept His remedy for sin. God's remedy to is accept Christ's forgiveness of your sins by trusting your life to Him, and trying to live the Christian life through God's Spirit from now on. There's a big difference between being sorry when you get caught at sinning and being sorry you're a sinner. Only this last expression is genuine, saving, godly repentance. (See chapter 2 and 3.)

- **Miracle-working demons**—Do you think every miracle you see or hear about is from God? *It isn't!* The devil and his demons can perform many so-called miracles and fool people into thinking these are signs from God! Be very careful when you rely on miracles as a proof that God works in the world. He does work, but you're to live by faith—not by trust in miracles and signs. (See chapters 3, 12, 13 & 17 and I Kings 22:21-23.)

Getting to know Jesus!

- *'The Holy One who is, and always was!'*—(see chapter 1)

- *Lord God Almighty*—(see chapter 1)

Nuts to crack—terms to know!

- **Wrath**—great anger!

- **Beast**—(see chapter 13)

- **Statue**—(see chapter 13)

- **Prophets**—(see chapters 1 & 18)

- **Plagues**—diseases. Many of these punishments are similar to the ones God brought upon the Egyptians in the days of Moses. (See Exodus 7-10; 32:35; Deut. 28:15, 27, 35.)

- **Cursed the name of God**—The word is blaspheme. The world will keep cursing God until the very end. (See chapter 13.)

- **Euphrates River**—The Euphrates River is 1780 miles long and extremely deep. It has always marked the boundary line between Eurasia and the people of the Orient. Perhaps the drying up of this great river will provide the way for the armies of the Orient to come to the Battle of Armageddon. God has dried up rivers before. (See Ex. 14:15-16; Josh. 4:7-8.)

- **Kings from the East!**—These kings may lead armies from Hell or from Earth, we can't be sure. If they lead earthly armies, it could refer to China. 'Kings of the east' actually means *kings of the sun rising.*

- **Three evil spirits that looked like frogs!**—The reference to frogs may mean something unclean. Why are there three? No one knows.

- **Dragon**—(see chapters 2 & 12)

- **False Prophet**—(see the 'two beasts' in chapter 13)

- **Armageddon!**—This means 'hill of Megiddo' and means a place in northern Israel. Armageddon stands for a great and awesome battle between good and evil. This is considered the final showdown between God and the devil at the end of history.

- **"It is finished!"**—With this judgment, God's punishment on a sinful world is completed. In completing the payment for such punishment (for those who would accept Him), Jesus said the same words on the cross. (See John 19:30!)

- **Demons**—(see chapter 9)

- **Babylon**—(see chapter 14)

Backpack for the road—Principles to Ponder!

- *People become more of what they are over time—either good or bad!*—Have you ever noticed that really old people seem either very, very nice, or very, very mean? Over time, people just become more and more what they already are—better or worse. In the next world, there's no time. That world lasts forever—eternal Heaven or eternal Hell. In Hell, wicked people will continue to get more wicked, while in Heaven, the righteous and holy people will continue to become more holy. (See chapters 9 & 22:11, and Dan. 12:10; Psalms 95:6-11; Prov. 28:14; Heb. 3:12-13.)

- *You reap what you sow*—What goes around comes around! (See chapter 2.)

- *Everything God does is right—never forget that!*—Even though God doesn't always tell you why He lets trouble and disappointment come into your life, never forget—He's in control. He allows these for a purpose. Somehow, if you trust Him, God will work out for good even the troubles in your life. Someday He'll explain to you His reasoning, but for now, just trust and obey. God is holy and can never do anything that is wrong. Remember that. (See chapter 8 and Gen. 50:20; Rom. 8:28.)

Journal for the journey—My reflections!

- ✓ The last time I didn't get away with something wrong, was I more sorry about what I *did*, or because I *got caught* at it?

- ✓ Am I paying attention in the news to the rise in power of China?

- ✓ Do I listen to the news to see how God is working in my world?

- ✓ How am I growing in Christ? Am I becoming more like Christ, or the world?

- ✓ *Life is rough. We all have tough times!* How is this statement different for Christians and non-Christians?

- ✓ Do I find comfort in knowing that God has my best interest at heart when He permits bad things to happen in my life?

- ✓ How do I *really* feel when evil people get what they deserve? Is this wrong? How do I know?

- ✓ What does Jesus mean when He says He will return *"as unexpectedly as a thief?"* (See I Thes. 5:2-4; 4:13-18.) How should this affect the way I *act* and *speak* every day?

Chapter 17

"The Church of the Unholy Prostitute!"
('You mean religion can be a bad thing?')

_1_ One of the seven angels who had poured out the seven bowls came over and spoke to me. "Come with me," he said, "and I will show you the judgment that is going to come on the great prostitute, who sits on many waters. _2_ The rulers of the world have had immoral relations with her, and the people who belong to this world have been made drunk by the wine of her immorality." _3_ So the angel took me in spirit into the wilderness. There I saw a woman sitting on a scarlet beast that had seven heads and ten horns, written all over with blasphemies against God. _4_ The woman wore purple and scarlet clothing and beautiful jewelry made of gold and precious gems and pearls. She held in her hand a gold goblet full of obscenities and the impurities of her immorality. _5_ A mysterious name was written on her forehead: "Babylon the Great, Mother of All Prostitutes and Obscenities in the World." _6_ I could see that she was drunk—drunk with the blood of God's holy people who were witnesses for Jesus. I stared at her completely amazed. _7_ "Why are you so amazed?" the angel asked. "I will tell you the mystery of this woman and of the beast with seven heads and ten horns. _8_ The beast you saw was alive but isn't now. And yet he'll soon come up out of the bottomless pit and go to eternal destruction. And the people who belong to this world, whose names were not written in the Book of Life from before the world began, will be amazed at the reappearance of this beast who had died. _9_ "And now understand this: The seven heads of the beast represent the seven hills of the city where this woman rules. They also represent seven kings. _10_ Five kings have already fallen, the sixth now reigns, and the seventh is yet to come, but his reign will be brief. _11_ The beast that was alive and then died is the eighth king. He is like the other seven, and he, too, will go to his doom. _12_ His ten horns are ten kings who have not yet risen to power; they will be appointed to their kingdoms for one brief moment to reign with the beast. _13_ They will all agree to give their power and authority to him. _14_ Together they will wage war against the Lamb, but the Lamb will defeat them because he is Lord over all lords and King over all kings, and his people are the called and chosen and faithful ones." *15* And the angel said to me, "The waters where the prostitute is sitting represent masses of people of every nation and language. *16* The beast and his ten horns—which represent ten kings who will reign with him—all hate the prostitute. They will strip her naked, eat her flesh, and burn her remains with fire. *17* For God has put a plan into their minds, a plan that will carry out his purposes. They will mutually agree to give their authority to the beast, and so the words of God will be fulfilled. *18* And this woman you saw in your vision means the great city that rules over the kings of the earth."

Explained in a nutshell!

There's a great timeout in *Revelation* as John is shown the two great influences in the world—religion and government—and what becomes of them. Religion is trying to reach God apart from Jesus Christ. Religion is seen as a powerful force that has influenced every world empire. On the surface, religion appears noble and glorious. But in its heart—without Christ—God sees it as empty and disgusting. Because it only serves to please mankind, and is missing the genuine love of Christ that truly leads to God, God calls it a prostitute. Religion is Buddhism, Islam, Hinduism, Kabbalah, Mormonism, Humanism, Scientology—every effort to reach God apart from Christ. Next, an angel explains the governmental system of the world—ruled by Satan through the Beast (Antichrist) in the end times. The Beast may attempt a fake resurrection from the dead in order to copy Jesus. Satan has influenced the governments of the seven great world powers which have come against Israel. In the Great Tribulation, the Beast will gather ten final nations of earth together against God. United, the world's final government will turn against and destroy the religions of the world and call Antichrist alone *god*. But God knows the end from the beginning, and will destroy both Antichrist and his united armies.

Key verse: 17:17

Key word: Immorality

Focus locus—themes and threads throughout!

- **Religion and Christianity are different!**—Someone has said that religion is what you do to reach God, but Christianity is what God has already done to reach you. Religion says we're all one world with one

'Father God' figure. Christianity says the world is two—those saved in Christ and those lost without Him. Only Christians have the right to call God their Heavenly Father. Christianity and religion aren't the same. Christianity is a change of your whole personhood into Christ-likeness. The world is very much into religion. Religions such as Islam, Scientology, and Mormonism are very popular right now. Religion is loving others, doing deeds of charity, accepting differences in people, going to church, etc. These are not bad things to do. In fact, they're great! But nothing you can do will forgive the sin problem every person suffers from. Religion is useless for forgiveness. No matter how many good things you do, the sin problem is still there. God sent His Son Jesus to settle the sin problem. Only an action like the death of the Son of God could cure the sin problem. Any other method is hopeless, which is why most of the world will die outside God's saving grace. (See chapter 20 and Prov. 14:12; Acts 4:12.)

- Dying for your faith!—(see 'martyr' in chapter 2)

Getting to know Jesus!

- *Lamb*—Jesus (see chapters 5 & 12).

- *'Lord of lords and King of kings!'*—This is the grandest title for Christ in all of *Revelation!* When He comes to rule and reign upon the earth at His Second Coming, His power and greatness will make Him the most magnificent ruler the world has ever known!

Nuts to crack—terms to know!

- **Mother of all prostitutes and obscenities**—This woman is a harlot. A harlot is a woman whose affection is false. A harlot is a prostitute. Prostitutes very often like to dress in red—the color of passion. Again, the reference is to false religion—the religion that makes life easy and requires no sacrifice of Christ—religion that looks good from the outside, but in reality is false and has nothing to do with Christianity. Religion that is unfaithful to the teachings of Jesus isn't acceptable to God! This harlot may stand for all the false religions of the world!

- **Scarlet beast**—The beast on which the woman sits is also scarlet (red). This could refer to the great number of deaths the world's false religions have caused. The color red could also refer to the royal but filthy conduct that false religion has taken part in all through history.

- **'Many waters'**—Since waters can refer to the many people and nations of the world, we see this false religion controlling many people on earth. It is a religion based on conduct and money—not faith and trust in God.

- **Immoral relations/immorality**—(see chapter 14)

- **Seven heads**—(see chapter 13)

- **Ten horns**—(see chapter 13)

- **Seven kings**—In *Revelation*, seven is the number of completeness. These are seven kings, or world empires, which have been linked to the nation Israel since Old Testament days. They are Egypt, Assyria, Babylon, Greece, Persia, Rome, and whatever the final great empire of earth will be at history's end. These also refer to the city of 'seven hills'—known by all as Rome. Perhaps Rome will be the center of false religion during this time. In these kings or kingdoms, God shows that after *seventh* one, the list is finished.

- **Blaspheme**—(see chapter 13 & 16)

- **The gold goblet**—This expresses the royal appearance of sinfulness. Satan makes it look good—not bad. If sinfulness appeared to you as the awful evil it was, you might never choose to sin. It also shows that God notices all sins. He doesn't let them slip by, because God is holy. Sin must be punished. God's plan is for all the sins of the world to be *collected*, and to be dealt with at the right time. In *Revelation*, the right time has now arrived.

- **Holy people**—These are called saints. (see chapter 8)

- **Witnesses**—also called *martyrs* (see chapter 2)

- **Mystery**—(see chapter 1)

- **Beast**—(see chapter 13)

- **Bottomless pit**—A reference to Hell, or one of the dark chambers of the underworld. Wherever it is, you would not want to see the evil creatures that live there! (See chapter 20.)

- **Eternal destruction/doom**—Generally means Hell. (See chapters 2, 9, 14, 19 and 20.)

- **Book of Life**—(see chapter 3)

- **The 'city'**—We can't be sure of what city this means. Many people think the city is Rome.

Backpack for the road—Principles to Ponder!

- *God's kids will seldom ever be fooled by the devil for very long!*—The devil will fool most of the world during the Great Tribulation. The world will think Antichrist is the savior who will finally bring peace to Planet Earth. But people who become Christians during this awful time will be led by God's Spirit, and know what's of God and what's not. It's the same today. While it's sometimes hard to separate religion from real Christianity, if you follow the Spirit of God in your heart—and the Bible in your backpack—you won't fall for the devil's tricks. At least not for long. (See chapters 3, 12, 13 & 16 and Matt. 24:24; John 10:4-5.)

- *Even though you're free to make your choices, God uses them for His purpose!*—*Revelation* makes it clear that God is sovereign. That is, everything happens according to His plan and will. But sometimes He performs those plans through our own free choices. This isn't easy to understand. Just know that God controls the choices you're perfectly free to make. He can even turn your bad choices into good, because He is in charge of the future. This doesn't mean it's OK to make bad choices. Sometimes you'll have to pay for those choices. It does mean that when you do, you can trust God to turn your lemons into lemonade. (See chapters 4, 10 and 11.)

Journal for the journey—My reflections!

- ✓ Why do most people think they're going to Heaven because of their good deeds? Can good deeds earn you a way to heaven? How many good deeds would it take?

✓ *Some people accept Jesus as Savior but not as Lord.* Explain why you agree or disagree with this statement. Do you think it makes a difference to God?

✓ How can I be *sure* I'm faithful to Christ's teachings?

✓ Why does sin usually appear as something beautiful and good rather than something evil and ugly?

✓ What do you see in your world that looks like fun or good to most people, but God would consider sinful?

✓ Has God ever put a plan in your mind that would let you to carry out His will?

Chapter 18

"Wall Street's Greatest Crash!"
(Or, 'don't get *too* attached to your toys!')

1 After all this I saw another angel come down from Heaven with great authority, and the earth grew bright with his splendor. *2* He gave a mighty shout, "Babylon is fallen—that great city is fallen! She has become the hideout of demons and evil spirits, a nest for filthy buzzards, and a den for dreadful beasts. *3* For all the nations have drunk the wine of her passionate immorality. The rulers of the world have committed adultery with her, and merchants throughout the world have grown rich as a result of her luxurious living." *4* Then I heard another voice calling from Heaven, "Come away from her, my people. Do not take part in her sins, or you'll be punished with her. *5* For her sins are piled as high as Heaven, and God is ready to judge her for her evil deeds. *6* Do to her as she has done to your people. Give her a double penalty for all her evil deeds. She brewed a cup of terror for others, so give her twice as much as she gave out. *7* She has lived in luxury and pleasure, so match it now with torments and sorrows. She boasts, 'I am queen on my throne. I am no helpless widow. I won't experience sorrow.' *8* Therefore, the sorrows of death and mourning and famine will overtake her in a single day. She'll be utterly consumed by fire, for the Lord God who judges her is mighty." *9* And the rulers of the world who took part in her immoral acts and enjoyed her great luxury will mourn for her as they see the smoke rising from her charred remains. *10* They will stand at a distance, terrified by her great torment. They will cry out, "How terrible, how terrible for Babylon, that great city! In one single moment God's judgment came on her." *11* The merchants of the world will weep and mourn for her, for there is no one left to buy their goods. *12* She bought great quantities of gold, silver, jewels, pearls, fine linen, purple dye, silk, scarlet cloth, every kind of perfumed wood, ivory goods, objects made of expensive wood, bronze, iron, and marble. *13* She also bought cinnamon, spice, incense, myrrh, frankincense, wine, olive oil, fine flour, wheat, cattle, sheep, horses, chariots, and slaves—yes, she even traded in human lives.

_14_ "All the fancy things you loved so much are gone," they cry. "The luxuries and splendor that you prized so much will never be yours again. They are gone forever." _15_ The merchants who became wealthy by selling her these things will stand at a distance, terrified by her great torment. They will weep and cry. _16_ "How terrible, how terrible for that great city! She was so beautiful—like a woman clothed in finest purple and scarlet linens, decked out with gold and precious stones and pearls! _17_ And in one single moment all the wealth of the city is gone!" And all the ship owners and captains of the merchant ships and their crews will stand at a distance. _18_ They will weep as they watch the smoke ascend, and they will say, "Where in all the world is there another city like this?" _19_ And they will throw dust on their heads to show their great sorrow. And they will say, "How terrible, how terrible for the great city! She made us all rich from her great wealth. And now in a single hour it is all gone." _20_ But you, O Heaven, rejoice over her fate. And you also rejoice, O holy people of God and apostles and prophets! For at last God has judged her on your behalf. _21_ Then a mighty angel picked up a boulder as large as a great millstone. He threw it into the ocean and shouted, "Babylon, the great city, will be thrown down as violently as I have thrown away this stone, and she'll disappear forever. _22_ Never again will the sound of music be heard there—no more harps, songs, flutes, or trumpets. There will be no industry of any kind, and no more milling of grain. _23_ Her nights will be dark, without a single lamp. There will be no happy voices of brides and grooms. This will happen because her merchants, who were the greatest in the world, deceived the nations with her sorceries. _24_ In her streets the blood of the prophets was spilled. She was the one who slaughtered God's people all over the world."

Explained in a nutshell!

John has seen the end of world religion and world government. Still in the tribulation timeout, he's now shown the end of world finance. The world's love for money and goods is seen as a haven for every kind of wickedness. Even God's own people have to be called away from this system of love for worldly luxury! As wealth and luxury ruined so many who loved and trusted it, so this system will itself be ruined in the end times. The 'Wall Street'  of the world will crash with great suddenness. Everyone will be amazed. The rich will weep as God turns out the lights of world finance, world religion, and world government at the end of the Great Tribulation. The stage is set for the brightness of the Second Coming of Jesus!

Key verse: 18:14

Key word: gone forever

Focus locus—themes and threads throughout!

- **Living holy and 'separate' from sin!**—(see *holy* in chapter 4) You live in the world, but you'd do well not to let the evil ways of the world live in you. The word separate is actually the word *holy*. When you live separate from the world it doesn't mean you live perfect and never sin. It means you live pure and ask forgiveness for the sins you commit. (See chapters 2, 13 & 14 and II Cor. 6:17.)

- **God's judgment!**—(see chapters 2, 3 & 11)

- **Repentance**—(see chapters 2, 3 and 16)

Nuts to crack—terms to know!

- **Babylon**—(see chapter 14)

- **Plagues**—Diseases.

- **'One single day'**—This means the speed with which destruction happens!

- **'One single moment'**—Again, the destruction will come suddenly!

- **Frankincense**—A very fragrant and costly spice.

- **Passionate immorality/immoral acts**—(see chapter 14)

- **Apostles**—(see chapter 2)

- **Prophet**—A prophet is someone who speaks for God. They deliver God's message. Sometimes they predicted the future, but usually they just preached.

- **Millstone**—This was a large stone used to crush grain. A millstone was very heavy.

Backpack for the road—Principles to Ponder!

- *How much you love the things of the world is measured by how sad you are when those things are gone!*—God put you in the world to enjoy its blessings, but not to enjoy its sins. Sometimes you can get too attached to the things of this world. How much you miss them when they're gone is a measure of your love. Be sure you don't get too attached. Notice that these people weep over their *loss*, not their *sin*. Someday you'll die and leave everything behind. Only what you do for Christ will last into the next life. (See Luke 12:20; I John 2:15; I Tim. 6:6-10; Matt. 6:21; James 5:1-6; II Cor. 6:14-18.)

- *What goes around comes around! Be careful what you do and say!*—(see chapter 2)

- *God's judgment is always fair, even if doesn't seem to be sometimes!*— God sees things—including the future—much more clearly than you and I do. He is also much more holy. Sometimes you wonder why God does what He does. Sometimes bad things happen to good people, and it seems unfair. Always remember that God can't be unholy or unfair— even when you don't understand His ways. (See chapter 3 and Nah. 1:2-3; II Thes.1:6-10; Rom. 11:22; I Cor. 10-1-12; II Pet. 3:3-7.)

Journal for the journey—My reflections!

- ✓ What worldly things do I hold on to most tightly? How would I feel if God took these away from me?

- ✓ *The bigger they are, the harder they fall.* How does this expression apply here?

- ✓ Do I notice any similarities between *America* and the Babylon of this chapter?

- ✓ Is there any worldly activity that God would ask me to *come out of* right now?

- ✓ Why does God sometimes wait so long to act?

- ✓ How can I live in a sinful world without letting a sinful world live in *me*?

- ✓ Does my enjoyment of 'stuff' such as sports, MP-3 players, Play Stations, CD's, movies, cars, video games, computers, etc., get in the way of my relationship with God?

- ✓ Even though I've given my life to God, am I also giving Him my *time*?

Chapter 19

"The Second Coming of Jesus"
(*The Return of the King*—not the movie!)

1 After this, I heard the sound of a vast crowd in Heaven shouting, "Hallelujah! Salvation is from your God. Glory and power belong to him alone. *2* His judgments are just and true. He has punished the great prostitute who corrupted the earth with her immorality, and he has avenged the murder of his servants." *3* Again and again their voices rang, "Hallelujah! The smoke from that city ascends forever and forever!" *4* Then the twenty-four elders and the four living beings fell down and worshiped God, who was sitting on the throne. They cried out, "Amen! Hallelujah!" *5* And from the throne came a voice that said, "Praise your God, all his servants, from the least to the greatest, all who fear him." *6* Then I heard again what sounded like the shout of a huge crowd, or the roar of mighty ocean waves, or the crash of loud thunder: "Hallelujah! For the Lord your God, the Almighty, reigns. *7* Let us be glad and rejoice and honor him. For the time has come for the wedding feast of the Lamb, and his bride has prepared herself. *8* She is permitted to wear the finest white linen." (Fine linen means the good deeds done by the people of God.) *9* And the angel said, "Write this: Blessed are those who are invited to the wedding feast of the Lamb." And he added, "These are true words that come from God." *10* Then I fell down at his feet to worship him, but he said, "No, don't worship me. For I am a servant of God, just like you and other brothers and sisters who testify of their faith in Jesus. Worship God. For the essence of prophecy is to give a clear witness for Jesus." *11* Then I saw Heaven opened, and a white horse was standing there. And the one sitting on the horse was named Faithful and True. For he judges fairly and then goes to war. *12* His eyes were bright like flames of fire, and on his head were many crowns. A name was written on him, and only he knew what it meant. *13* He was clothed with a robe dipped in blood, and his title was the Word of God. *14* The armies of Heaven, dressed in pure white linen, followed him on white horses. *15* From his mouth came a sharp sword, and with it he struck down the nations. He ruled them with an iron rod, and he trod the winepress of the fierce wrath of almighty God. *16* On his robe and thigh was written this title: King of kings and Lord of lords. *17* Then I saw an angel standing in the sun, shouting to the vultures flying high in the sky: "Come! Gather together for the great banquet God has prepared. *18* Come and eat the flesh of kings, captains, and strong warriors; of horses and their riders; and of all humanity, both free and slave, small and great." *19* Then I saw the beast gathering the kings of the earth and their armies in order to fight against the one sitting on the horse and his army. *20* And the beast was captured, and with him the false prophet who did mighty miracles on behalf of the beast—miracles that deceived all who had accepted the mark of the beast and who worshiped his statue. Both the beast and his false prophet were thrown alive into the lake of fire that burns with sulfur. *21* Their entire army was killed by the sharp sword that came out of the mouth of the one riding the white horse. And all the vultures of the sky gorged themselves on the dead bodies.

Explained in a nutshell!

The world systems have collapsed. Over half the population of the world has died. The environment has been wrecked. Antichrist and his armies turn their weapons against Almighty God in Heaven. But Heaven rejoices and praises God! The end of the Great Tribulation has arrived, and the time for great celebration has come! Here in Heaven, Christians will be wed to Jesus—their Bridegroom—at the grandest Wedding Feast of all time! Jesus will now receive the honor and glory He has always deserved. The Heavens split open, and Jesus returns to earth followed by the angel armies of Heaven and the Christians of all ages! Christ and Antichrist—the final battle of good and evil. It will be the last great bloodbath as the armies of earth are destroyed in an instant. The birds feast on the corpses! Antichrist and the False Prophet, however, have special treatment—they are thrown alive into Hell!

Key verse: 19:11

Key word: Hallelujah

Focus locus—themes and threads throughout!

- **Living holy**—(see chapter 4)

- **Heaven**—(see chapter 4)

- **Hell**—(see chapters 2, 9 & 20)

- **The Second Coming of Jesus**—This is the great event that ends history as we know it. It's the point toward which all of *Revelation* has been heading. The first coming of Jesus was as a baby in Bethlehem. He grew to manhood in Jerusalem and died on a cross to pay for your sins. His own people (the Jews) rejected Him as their Savior, so Jesus ascended (see chapter 11) back to Heaven. When Jesus comes the second time, He'll come as a King of Heaven and earth. He'll judge sin and sinful people, and put an end to evil, Antichrist, and the devil's control over earth's affairs. When He comes the second time, the Jewish people will accept Him as their Savior, and He'll set up His kingdom on earth and bring peace to mankind. (See chapters 1 & 12, and Matt. 24:27-31; Zech. 12:10-11; 13:6; 14:3-13; Isa. 49:15-16; 63:1-6; Cp. Acts 1:9-11; Jude 14-15.)

Getting to know Jesus!

- *Salvation*—What an appropriate name for Jesus. His name Jesus (in Hebrew) means salvation! (See chapters 7 and 14.)

- *The Lord your God*—(see chapter 1)

- *The Almighty*—(see chapter 1)

- *King of Kings & Lord of Lords!*—(see chapter 17; Cp. Deut. 10:17; Ps. 136:3; I Tim. 6:15.)

- *The Lamb*—(see chapter 5)

- *The Essence of prophecy*—Jesus is called the Word of God. What Jesus says is what God says. The Bible is also the Word of God. It's how God speaks to us today. Since 'prophesy' (see chapter 10) means *to speak for God*, Jesus is the very heart and soul of what God has to tell us. Listen to Him through the Bible. Follow Him through your actions and words. Remember, you're the only Bible some people will ever read.

- *Faithful & True*—(see chapters 1 & 3)

- *The Word of God!*—As we've seen, Jesus is the very Word of God. When you read your Bible (the Word of God too), you're reading the instructions of God Himself! (See John 1:1; Col. 2:9.)

- *The 'new, unknown name!'*—Names were extremely important in ancient times (see chapters 2 & 3). When Jesus returns to the earth as Lord and King, He'll have a new name—a very holy and special name—which maybe only God Himself will understand. You'll have a new name, too, but we'll get to that later. (See John 10:15.)

Nuts to crack—terms to know!

- Hallelujah—A very special Hebrew word which means *to praise the Lord*. Notice that all heaven praises God for four things: His *salvation*, His *justice*, His *holiness*, and His *awesomeness*! Can't you hear Handel's *Messiah* here? (See Psalms 97; Cp. Rev. 5:13-14; 7:9-12; 11:15-18.)

- Immorality—(see chapter 14)

- The twenty-four Elders & four Living beings—(see chapter 4)

- Amen—(see chapter 3)

- Omnipotent—This is the God of all power! (see chapters 1, 4 & 6)

- The wedding feast of the Lamb—At the Second Coming of Christ, there's going to be a marriage! Well, it's called a marriage, but it's more like a very special banquet where Jesus and all Christians finally meet face to face—never to be separated again. At this wedding, Christians may receive the rewards Jesus has for us mentioned in I Cor. 3:10-15. *Rewards*—not *salvation*—are the subject of that passage. (Cp. Matt. 25:14-46; II Cor. 5:9-10; Col. 3:23-25.)

- Fine linen—(see 'garments' in chapter 3)

- **Christians are called Christ's 'Bride'**—The picture here is of beauty, purity, and love. It will be the mother of all celebrations! Think of the love you'll share with the One who died to save you from your sins, and made spending forever in Heaven possible! Think of the largest banquet you've ever been to. This one will be thousands of times greater! What a reunion it will be, too—all your friends and relatives who were Christians will be there. So will many of the great heroes you've read about in the Bible—and in history. (See Eph. 5:25-27; II Cor. 11:2-3.)

- **Sharp sword**—(See chapter 1.)

- **Rod of iron**—(see chapter 2; Cp. Isa. 9:6-7; Psalms 2:9.)

- **Winepress**—(see chapter 14)

- **The great banquet God has prepared**—While the Marriage Supper will be a grand and joyous celebration in Heaven, on Earth there will be another supper. This supper isn't a pleasant one. As the Great Tribulation ends, there will be so much death and destruction that the birds of the air will be feasting on the flesh of the dead. While you must be a Christian, and have an invitation to attend the Wedding Feast, the only requirement for being a 'part' of this 'banquet' is to be *unsaved* at the Battle of Armageddon. (See Matt. 24:28-29.)

- **Crowns**—Jesus is seen wearing *many* crowns here. (See Rev. 2.)

- **Beast & False Prophet**—(see chapter 13)

- **Mark**—(see chapter 13)

- **Statue**—(see chapter 13)

- **Lake of Fire**—A description of Hell. Think of the awful pain of fire without ever being able to die! Suffering without end—that's what Hell is! (See chapters 2 & 9.)

- **Burning sulphur**—Called brimstone. (See chapters 9 & 14.)

Backpack for the road—Principles to Ponder!

- *Redemption is costly*—The price is *death!* (See chapters 5 and 6.)

Journal for the journey—My reflections!

- ✓ Have I ever hoped Jesus wouldn't return soon so that I could do some things I wanted to do in life? Was this wrong? Why? Why not?

- ✓ How would I answer someone who said the Bible was *not* the Word of God?

- ✓ If I could choose a one-word description of myself for my new name which God will give me someday, what would it be? Why did you choose that one?

- ✓ Will there be animals in Heaven?

- ✓ What will be the first three questions I want to ask Jesus?

- ✓ Who do I *most* want to meet in Heaven?

Chapter 20

"One Cool Kingdom to Come!"
(Perfect world—frightening judgment!)

_1_ Then I saw an angel come down from Heaven with the key to the bottomless pit and a heavy chain in his hand. _2_ He seized the dragon—that old serpent, the Devil, Satan—and bound him in chains for a thousand years. _3_ The angel threw him into the bottomless pit, which he then shut and locked so Satan could not deceive the nations anymore until the thousand years were finished. Afterward he would be released again for a little while. _4_ Then I saw thrones, and the people sitting on them had been given the authority to judge. And I saw the souls of those who had been beheaded for their testimony about Jesus, for proclaiming the word of God. And I saw the souls of those who had not worshiped the beast or his statue, nor accepted his mark on their forehead or their hands. They came to life again, and they reigned with Christ for a thousand years. _5_ This is the first resurrection. (The rest of the dead did not come back to life until the thousand years had ended.) _6_ Blessed and holy are those who share in the first resurrection. For them the second death holds no power, but they will be priests of God and of Christ and will reign with him a thousand years. _7_ When the thousand years end, Satan will be let out of his prison. _8_ He'll go out to deceive the nations from every corner of the earth, which are called Gog and Magog. He'll gather them together for battle—a mighty host, as numberless as sand along the shore. _9_ And I saw them as they went up on the broad plain of the earth and surrounded God's people and the beloved city. But fire from Heaven came down on the attacking armies and consumed them. _10_ Then the Devil, who betrayed them, was thrown into the lake of fire that burns with sulfur, joining the beast and the false prophet. There they will be tormented day and night forever and ever. _11_ And I saw a great white throne, and I saw the one who was sitting on it. The earth and sky fled from his presence, but they found no place to hide. _12_ I saw the dead, both great and small, standing before God's throne. And the books were opened, including the Book of Life. And the dead were judged according to the things written in the books, according to what they had done. *13* The sea gave up the dead in it, and death and the grave gave up the dead in them. They were all judged according to their deeds. *14* And death and the grave were thrown into the lake of fire. This is the second death—the lake of fire. *15* And anyone whose name was not found recorded in the Book of Life was thrown into the lake of fire.

Explained in a nutshell!

Have you ever wondered what the perfect world would be like? What would Earth be like with the perfect ruler, and sin unable to bring evil and destruction? Such a world is coming! John now sees the setting up of Christ's earthly kingdom. The devil is chained in Hell for 1000 years, and peace finally reigns on earth. In Heaven, John sees those killed by Antichrist for their faith during the Great Tribulation. These are given rulership in the kingdom, along with all the righteous dead of all time. Many of the survivors from the Great Tribulation are also allowed to enter the kingdom, and will have many children. After the 1000 years are over, God releases Satan to test the children born in the kingdom. He gathers many of them against God, but they are destroyed and sent forever to Hell. At last, the Great White Throne judgment of the lost from all the ages of history takes place. Each person is judged by his or her works. Every good and bad thing these people ever did will be discussed. Their works can't save them apart from Christ, and they—along with death itself—are sent to Hell. Forever.

Key verse: 20:12

Key word: Judged

Focus locus—themes and threads throughout!

- Hell is forever!—(see chapters 2, 9 & 20)

- The Kingdom of Christ!—A king must have a kingdom. At His Second Coming to earth, Jesus will set up His kingdom of peace on Earth, which will last 1000 years! This is the kingdom the ancient Jewish people expected the Messiah to bring. They didn't see Jesus as their Savior because He didn't bring it at once. In this kingdom, every person that ever lived who put his or her faith and trust in God will live. You'll have a part too. Your talents and gifts will be put to good use. The earth will

be changed as Christ *redeems* the earth! (See chapters 5, 6, 14 and 22.) First, most evil will be gone since the devil will be locked up! Second, nature will be more like it was in the Garden of Eden. Plants and trees will be far more beautiful—and they may not ever die! Third, even the animals will be changed. They won't fear man as many do today, and the lion and the lamb will sit together in peace! The desire to kill and destroy will be gone! What a wonderful kingdom this will be! Many people who are not killed in the Great Tribulation will populate Christ's kingdom in their natural bodies. This means that some of them will actually give birth! While most of us won't be in physical bodies, those who are will live much longer than people do today. The kingdom will be like a Heaven on earth for 1000 years! (See Acts 3:21; Rom. 8:19-23.) (For characteristics of God's Kingdom on earth, see Isa. 2:3; 11:6-8; 32:15-18; 33:17-24; 35:3-7; 65:20-23; Zech. 8:22-23; 14:16-19; Joel 2:21-29; Ezek. 36:8-11.)

- **Resurrection**—(see chapters 1 & 11)

- **God's judgment!**—(see chapters 2, 3 & 11)

Nuts to crack—terms to know!

- **Key**—Authority (see chapter 1)

- **Bottomless pit**—(see chapter 17)

- **Dragon, Satan, devil!**—(see chapters 2& 12)

- **1,000 years (millennium)**—see 'Kingdom of Christ'

- **Thrones**—Where kings sit.

- **Statue**—(see chapter 13)

- **The 'mark'**—(see chapter 13)

- **Testimony**—(see chapter 1)

- **Lived again**—This is resurrection—(see chapters 1 & 11)

- **The lake of fire!**—This is another description of Hell. (See chapters 2, 9, 14 and 19.)

- **The 'second death'**—(see chapter 2)

- **Gog & Magog**—These mysterious terms probably just refer to the farthest parts of the earth.

- **The 'Books'**—Maybe the books here are the Book of the Living (everyone who has ever lived), the Book of the Instructions for Eternal Life (the Bible), and the Lamb's Book of Life (the names of believers; see chapter 3).  We can't know for sure what all these books are. Maybe they will include records of all the *words* a person has ever spoken, as well as all their *good deeds*, and every *thought*. All we know for sure is that everyone here will suffer, and none are saved. (See John 12:48; Luke 12:47-48; Dan. 7:9-12; 12:1; Matt. 12:36.)

- **Book of Life**—(see chapter 3)

- **The 'city'**—Jerusalem.

- **The Great White Throne!**—This is the last judgment of mankind. It takes place in Heaven at the end of the 1000 years of Christ's earthly kingdom. We are told it's big, gleaming pure, and white, and the King of the Universe sits there. Gathered before God will be every person who has ever lived that did not put their faith and trust in God. Hitler will be here. Some of the most wicked people who ever lived will be here. Nice people will be here too. Why will nice people be at a judgment for people who will be sent to Hell? They will be there because this judgment isn't based on how nice a person was, or how many good things they did in life. This judgment is simply based on whether people put their life in God's hands and trusted Him by faith while they lived. Picture the millions and millions of people standing before a holy God. Picture them thinking their good deeds were enough to get them into Heaven. Picture Christ—the Great Judge—examining the books for their names. Finally, picture the looks on the faces of that great crowd when Christ can't find any of the names and tells each person: "I never knew you" and each person drops into Hell. Forever. (See II Cor.

11:15 and chapters 2, 9 & 17; John 5:22-27; Heb. 10:28-30; Matt. 22:13-14; 18:8-9; 25:46; Acts 10:42.)

- **The Grave**—Also referred to as Hades. Death and everything about death will finally be destroyed! (See I Cor. 15:26 and chapters 2, 6 & 9.)

Backpack for the road—Principles to Ponder!

- *Being good isn't enough for God. The standard is perfection!*—If we can't be perfect, then God can't let us into Heaven. Through Jesus, He made a way for all our sins to be forgiven, and for us to be perfect in His sight. If we accept Jesus, we can enter Heaven. This is why so many good people still aren't allowed into Heaven. Good? Yes. Perfect? No. (See chapter 17 and Rom. 3:10-18; Isa. 64:6.)

Journal for the journey—My reflections!

- ✓ What talents do I have that God might use in the Kingdom? Am I using them *now*?

- ✓ Why did God put the fear of mankind into the wild creatures in the first place?

- ✓ Why can't God just slip sinful people into Heaven based on their good deeds?

- ✓ How might I answer friends who say Heaven and Hell *don't* last forever?

- ✓ Why does God briefly release the devil at the end of the 1000 years?

- ✓ Why do the lost people have to stand before God and be judged if they're *already* lost?

- ✓ Is God being unfair when He lets people who've done many good things in the world go to the same Hell as murderers, rapists, and terrorists?

Chapter 21

"City Without a Cemetery!"
(Or, 'when the mother ship comes down to the earth!')

1 Then I saw a new Heaven and a new earth, for the old Heaven and the old earth had disappeared. And the sea was also gone. *2* And I saw the holy city, the new Jerusalem, coming down from God out of Heaven like a beautiful bride prepared for her husband. *3* I heard a loud shout from the throne, saying, "Look, the home of God is now among his people! He'll live with them, and they will be his people. God himself will be with them. *4* He'll remove all of their sorrows, and there will be no more death or sorrow or crying or pain. For the old world and its evils are gone forever." *5* And the one sitting on the throne said, "Look, I am making all things new!" And then he said to me, "Write this down, for what I tell you is trustworthy and true." *6* And he also said, "It is finished! I am the Alpha and the Omega—the Beginning and the End. To all who are thirsty I will give the springs of the water of life without charge! *7* All who are victorious will inherit all these blessings, and I will be their God, and they will be my children. *8* But cowards who turn away from me, and unbelievers, and the corrupt, and murderers, and the immoral, and those who practice witchcraft, and idol worshipers, and all liars—their doom is in the lake that burns with fire and sulfur. This is the second death." *9* Then one of the seven angels who held the seven bowls containing the seven last plagues came and said to me, "Come with me! I will show you the bride, the wife of the Lamb." *10* So he took me in spirit to a great, high mountain, and he showed me the holy city, Jerusalem, coming down out of Heaven from God. *11* It was filled with the glory of God and sparkled like a precious gem, crystal clear like jasper. *12* Its walls were broad and high, with twelve gates guarded by twelve angels. And the names of the twelve tribes of Israel were written on the gates. *13* There were three gates on each side—east, north, south, and west. *14* The wall of the city had twelve foundation stones, and on them were written the names of the twelve apostles of the Lamb. *15* The angel who talked to me held in his hand a gold measuring stick to measure the city, its gates, and its wall. _16_ When he measured it, he found it was a square, as wide as it was long. In fact, it was in the form of a cube, for its length and width and height were each 1,400 miles. _17_ Then he measured the walls and found them to be 216 feet thick (the angel used a standard human measure). _18_ The wall was made of jasper, and the city was pure gold, as clear as glass. _19_ The wall of the city was built on foundation stones inlaid with twelve gems: the first was jasper, the second sapphire, the third agate, the fourth emerald, _20_ the fifth onyx, the sixth carnelian, the seventh chrysolite, the eighth beryl, the ninth topaz, the tenth chrysoprase, the eleventh jacinth, the twelfth amethyst. _21_ The twelve gates were made of pearls—each gate from a single pearl! And the main street was pure gold, as clear as glass. _22_ No temple could be seen in the city, for the Lord God Almighty and the Lamb are its temple. _23_ And the city has no need of sun or moon, for the glory of God illuminates the city, and the Lamb is its light. _24_ The nations of the earth will walk in its light, and the rulers of the world will come and bring their glory to it. _25_ Its gates never close at the end of day because there is no night. _26_ And all the nations will bring their glory and honor into the city. _27_ Nothing evil will be allowed to enter—no one who practices shameful idolatry and dishonesty—but only those whose names are written in the Lamb's Book of Life.

Explained in a nutshell!

The 1000-year Kingdom of God is over. What happens beyond this is mostly a mystery. What we are told is that John sees a new Heaven and a new earth with no more oceans! Then, he is shown the New Jerusalem—a brilliant city-planet coming down to hover over the new earth. At last, God will dwell with His people, and pain, sorrow, and sinful people will be gone forever! God's plan is finished. Jesus reminds us that He is the eternal God, that He will meet our every need, and that evil people will go to Hell. Now John gets a tour of the New Jerusalem. It's nearly the size of the moon—a sphere possibly within a cube! The city gleams with beauty—so bright the sun and moon aren't needed! God's children will come and go there as they please, and there will be no night and no evil ever again.

Key verse: 20:4

Key word: New

Getting to know Jesus!

- *True and Faithful!*—(see chapters 1 & 3)

- *The Alpha & the Omega!*—(see chapter 1)
- *The Lord God Almighty*—(see chapter 1)
- *The Lamb*—(see chapter 5)

Nuts to crack—terms to know!

- **New Heaven & earth**—We know nothing except that God creates these. Exactly when and where? Nobody knows. What we *do* know is that since there will be no more sea, there will be *much* more room! It will also be holy, pure, and clean—*forever!* (See II Pet. 3:10-13.)

- **The New Jerusalem!**—This is a future Heavenly city. It seems to hover over a new Earth and is described as a beautiful place! The city flashes rainbow hues of red, blue, and green! It also sparkles as a diamond! We aren't told much about it, but it will be a gift of God to His children. It's a huge city, the size of the United States east of the Mississippi River! It's 1500 miles on each of its sides, is in the shape of a cube, and maybe fits inside a sphere! From the information given, it appears to be almost the size of the moon! The city has streets of gold, 12 pearly gates 300 miles apart, and walls 200 feet high! In this city, we find no night, no sea, and no need of artificial light. Neither will it have a cemetery! This city is so large that just the *first* floor of it is 10 times the size of Germany or France! On this floor alone, every person who has ever lived could fit, and the city could easily have *150,000 floors!* (See Heb. 11:10, 16; 12:10; 13:14; I Cor. 2:9.)

- **The springs of the water of life**—We don't know what these special waters are, but if they're Heavenly, they must be awesome! (See Psalms 63:1-8; John 4:13-14; 7:37-39.)

- **Witchcraft**—(see chapter 9)

- **Lake burning with fire & sulphur**—(see chapters 2, 9 & 19)

- **The 'second death'**—Separation forever from God. (See chapter 2.)

- **Plagues**—Diseases.

- **The Lamb's Book of Life**—A list of all the names of those who trusted in Christ (see chapters 3 & 17)

- **The Bride, the wife of the Lamb**—The bride is now called Christ's wife. She will have a honeymoon that will never end. (See 'marriage supper' in chapter 19.)

- **Golden measuring stick**—(see *reeds* chapter 11)

- **The pearl**—A pearl is the only precious stone that comes from a living creature—the oyster. The pearl is formed from a speck of sand that first hurts the oyster, and then forms into a most valuable gem! (See Matt. 13:45-46.)

- **Glory**—God's glory is the light and life of this city! It is mentioned three times here! (See John 1:14; 17:4-24; Rom. 8:17-18.)

Backpack for the road—Principles to Ponder!

- *Even in a perfect world, God remembers what we went through*—God shows this through the use of the pearl, whose beauty is only formed through distress and pain. (See chapter 4.)

Journal for the journey—My reflections!

✓ Why is there no sea in the New Jerusalem?

✓ Why does Jesus want me to inherit all *His* blessings?

✓ Just as the pearl is formed through the distress an oyster must endure, the difficulties God allows in your life can create beauty in your life, too. What difficulties have you had that have helped you become more 'beautiful' to God?

✓ If there are no tears or sorrow in heaven, does this mean you will not miss friends and family who won't make it there? What can you do right now to make sure they *do* make it?

Chapter 22

"Journey's End—Last Notes from Jesus..." (And you'd better not change *anything!*)

_1_ And the angel showed me a pure river with the water of life, clear as crystal, flowing from the throne of God and of the Lamb, _2_ coursing down the center of the main street. On each side of the river grew a tree of life, bearing twelve crops of fruit, with a fresh crop each month. The leaves were used for medicine to heal the nations. _3_ No longer will anything be cursed. For the throne of God and of the Lamb will be there, and his servants will worship him. _4_ And they will see his face, and his name will be written on their foreheads. _5_ And there will be no night there—no need for lamps or sun—for the Lord God will shine on them. And they will reign forever and ever. _6_ Then the angel said to me, "These words are trustworthy and true: 'The Lord God, who tells his prophets what the future holds, has sent his angel to tell you what will happen soon.'" _7_ "Look, I am coming soon! Blessed are those who obey the prophecy written in this scroll." _8_ I, John, am the one who saw and heard all these things. And when I saw and heard these things, I fell down to worship the angel who showed them to me. _9_ But again he said, "No, don't worship me. I am a servant of God, just like you and your brothers the prophets, as well as all who obey what is written in this scroll. Worship God!" _10_ Then he instructed me, "Do not seal up the prophetic words you have written, for the time is near. _11_ Let the one who is doing wrong continue to do wrong; the one who is vile, continue to be vile; the one who is good, continue to do good; and the one who is holy, continue in holiness." _12_ "See, I am coming soon, and my reward is with me, to repay all according to their deeds. _13_ I am the Alpha and the Omega, the First and the Last, the Beginning and the End." _14_ Blessed are those who wash their robes so they can enter through the gates of the city and eat the fruit from the tree of life. _15_ Outside the city are the dogs—the sorcerers, the sexually immoral, the murderers, the idol worshipers, and all who love to live a lie. _16_ "I, Jesus, have sent my angel to give you this message for the churches. I am both the source of David and the heir to his throne. I am the bright morning star." *17* The Spirit and the bride say, "Come." Let each one who hears them say, "Come." Let the thirsty ones come—anyone who wants to. Let them come and drink the water of life without charge. *18* And I solemnly declare to everyone who hears the prophetic words of this book: If anyone adds anything to what is written here, God will add to that person the plagues described in this book. *19* And if anyone removes any of the words of this prophetic book, God will remove that person's share in the tree of life and in the holy city that are described in this book. *20* He who is the faithful witness to all these things says, "Yes, I am coming soon!" Amen! Come, Lord Jesus! *21* The grace of the Lord Jesus be with you all.

Explained in a nutshell!

In the New Jerusalem, John sees a river flowing from God's throne through rows of ever-bearing fruit trees. The curse on God's creation is gone forever, and God dwells with His people. His glory shines so brightly there's no more night or darkness. *Revelation* ends. Its words about future events are holy and accurate. Jesus reminds us He is eternal and coming soon to reward every person according to their life. We're not to hide *Revelation*'s message, but are instructed to grow in the holiness by which God saved us, and look forward to the New Jerusalem prepared for us! No evil will ever be allowed in it! But for now, salvation through Jesus is still available to any who will accept it. The Book of *Revelation* ends with a strong warning against anyone who might change the words or message of the book.

Key verse: 22:6

Key word: Grace

Focus locus—themes and threads throughout!

- **The curse on planet Earth!**—Did you know that the earth today has a curse on it? No, not like a magical evil spell. Not that kind of curse. The curse on the earth is what causes aging and death of every living thing. God created a perfect world for Adam and Eve. Then, they gave in to the devil's temptation and sinned (disobeyed God). Sin came into the world through Adam and Eve, and brought aging and death to every living

thing—people, plants, and animals. Just think what life would have been like if Adam and Eve had not sinned! When He returns and sets up His kingdom (see chapter 20), Jesus will restore the earth to much like the world of Adam and Eve. But at the end of all things—in the very distant future known only to God—We won't have to worry about global warming, hurricanes, or the destruction of the environment. Earth will be totally new and perfect once again. Forever! The curse—and the sin that created it—will be history! (Cp. Rom. 8:19-23.)

- The Second Coming of Jesus!—(see chapters 1 & 19)

Getting to know Jesus!

- *The Lamb*—(see chapter 5)

- *The Lord God*—(see chapter 1)

- *The Alpha & Omega/First & Last/Beginning & End*—(see chapter 1)

- *The source of David & heir to his throne*—(see chapter 5)

- *The Bright & Morning Star!*—(see chapter 2)

- *Lord Jesus*

Nuts to crack—terms to know!

- Waters of Life—(see chapter 21)

- Tree of Life—(see chapter 2)

- Curse—Everything that sin has done to our universe will be forgotten forever! Death, pain, suffering, heartache, old age, sickness, disappointment—all gone! (See I Cor. 15:24-28.)

- Names—(see chapter 2, 3 and 19)

- Prophecy—(see chapter 1)

- Sealing—(see chapter 5)

- Rewards—(see 'crowns' in chapter 2)

- **Washing robes or garments**—(see chapters 3, 14 and 18)

- **Dogs**—Means anything that is unclean sexually. This term was sometimes used for homosexuals.

- **Sorcerers**—(see chapter 9)

- **Sexually immoral**—(see chapter 14)

- **Come**—the last invitation to be saved in the Bible! (See John 6:35; Isa. 55:1-3; Matt. 11:28.)

- **Plagues**—Diseases.

- **Grace**—*Amazing grace!* Salvation, which is free to you, cost God everything! (See Rom. 5:15-17; 6:23; Eph. 2:8-9; John 3:36; 12:36.)

Backpack for the road—Principles to Ponder!

- God's plan is bigger than anything you or I can imagine! His plan will succeed and not be interrupted by any force in the universe! One day, He'll have His perfect kingdom, and you and I—and every Christian who ever lived—will live there with Him forever! (See chapters 7, 10, 11, 13 & 19 and Isa. 55:8-9.)

Journal for the journey—My reflections!

✓ What can I do daily to spread the spirit of God's kingdom to those around me?

✓ How might I answer someone who says that *Revelation* can't be understood, and that I shouldn't spend time studying and worrying about it?

✓ Am I praying, witnessing, and studying the way God wants me to?

✓ What am I doing for Jesus that I'm *most* proud to go on doing?

✓ Am I ready if Jesus came today?

You've now come to the end of *Revelation*. How does it feel to have studied the very *last* thing God had to say to us? Now that you've finished *Dragons, Grasshoppers, & Frogs!*, here are some next steps you might want to consider:

- Make sure you've thoroughly reflected on the questions in the *Journal for the journey* sections.

- Pass *Dragons, Grasshoppers, & Frogs!* around to friends and family, and get a serious discussion about Jesus going!

- Get into a deeper study of *Revelation* by using commentaries such as the two listed at the front of this book. Maybe start a small group Bible study on *Revelation*.

- Watch the news and keep your eyes and ears open to events that remind you of what's to come!

Above all, remember that *Jesus* is the focus of *Revelation*. Not dragons, grasshoppers or frogs. If we take all the descriptions of Jesus from our *Getting to Know Jesus* sections, we see a most wonderful view of Him! Put into the form of a letter, His last message to you—from the last book of the Bible— might read something like this:

> "I am Jesus, your Faithful and Awesome Savior. I live forever! I have all power, and am timeless. I came to save you from your sins, and someday rule the world! I love you! I watch and correct you—my child—as your Father God. I know everything you do! Although I have power over all creation, and every nation on earth, my desire is to enter your heart. For this reason, I—the Mighty Lion—became a Sacrificial Lamb to die for your sins. One day, my power and judgment will be poured out against all evil! But today, I am also your Great Shepherd, watching over you, my sheep. I was born as a human child to die, defeat death, and one-day rule the world as Lord God Almighty and King of Kings. I, alone, am Salvation, God's final Word and Prophecy! My name is special. Remember me as the Eternal Lamb of God, the Lord Jesus, and the Morning star. Be looking for me. I'm coming back to take you home when you least expect me."
>
> —*Jesus*

Ten Things to watch for as the Time of *Revelation* Nears!

1. *Watch for trouble within Europe.* The European Union (EEC) won't stay together politically. France, Germany and Belgium are already drifting away from this union over the Iraq controversy. From this European shake-up will come the future *Antichrist.*

2. *Watch for evil people to get worse and worse.* The hearts of evil people will get more evil. Unspeakable crimes and violence will fill the evening news. *Terrorism* will spread throughout the world! Citizens will become more and more *angry* at the laws and police which are supposed to govern them.

3. *Watch for America to begin to pull away from Israel.* The *Palestinian* issue won't go away. *Anti-Semitism* will rise around the world. (The Holocaust was just a preview of worse things to come.) World and political pressures, as well as increasing oil prices, will eventually force America to weaken support for Israel.

4. *Watch for an increase in so-called 'supernatural miracles'.* Satan worship, witchcraft, drug use, and the occult will increase, and move more and more into the open. Miraculous conceptions, births, and 'healings' will show up on the evening news. Eventually, someone will claim to raise someone from the dead.

5. *Watch for Christianity to become more and more politically incorrect.* There will be less and less freedom to speak openly against things the Bible calls *sin* (homosexuality, abortion, etc.). *Tolerance* will increase in every area except *intolerance* of evil. Islam, Hinduism, and other religions that haven't been popular in America will take center-stage as Christianity declines.

6. *Watch for more and more inappropriate language in TV and in movies.* Sex, and *blasphemy against God* will become more and more tolerated.

7. *Watch for a spiritual famine in solid Bible teaching.* More and more people will say that man wrote the Bible without God's help. Emotion-devotion (the teaching that personal feelings matter more than Biblical facts), church growth, and the social/political gospel (the teaching that what we do to our fellow humans matters more than what we do with Jesus) will replace serious study of the Word of God.

8. *Watch for a rise in the power of the Far Eastern nations.* Keep a close eye on Korea, China, and Japan. Keep a close ear on the Tigris and Euphrates River areas.

9. *Watch for restless changes in nature.* There will be an increase in hurricanes, earthquakes and volcanic activity. More and more unusual things will appear on the land and in the sky.

10. *Watch for strange and unusual diseases to show up.* More and more there will be diseases that can't be cured, and they will be traced back to the wild animals of the earth.

About the Author

Jerry Parks teaches 7th grade social studies at Georgetown Middle School in Georgetown, Kentucky. He has three previously published works: *With Joseph in the University of Adversity: The Mizraim Principles*, a study of the life of Joseph the Hebrew, *So, You Want to be an NBPTS Certified Teacher?*, a guide for teachers considering the National Board Certification Process, and *Teacher Under Construction*, a handbook for new teachers. Jerry also teaches an *Adult Bible Fellowship* class at Southland Christian Church—one of the ten largest churches in America.

Made in the USA
Lexington, KY
03 April 2015